Country Roads
~ of ~
IDAHO

*A Guide Book
from Country Roads Press*

Country Roads
~ of ~
IDAHO

Bill London

Illustrated by
Cliff Winner

Country Roads Press
C A S T I N E • M A I N E

Country Roads of Idaho
© 1995 by Bill London. All rights reserved.

Published by Country Roads Press
P.O. Box 286, Lower Main Street
Castine, Maine 04421

Text and cover design by Edith Allard.
Cover illustration by Victoria Sheridan.
Illustrations by Cliff Winner.
Typesetting by Camden Type 'n Graphics.

ISBN 1-56626-069-8

Library of Congress Cataloging-in-Publication Data
London, Bill.
    Country Roads of Idaho / Bill London ; illustrator, Cliff
Winner.
        p. cm.
    Includes index.
    ISBN 1-56626-069-8 : $9.95
    1. Idaho—Tours. 2. Automobile travel—Idaho—
Guidebooks. I. Title.
    F744.3.L652   1995
    917.9604'33—dc20   94-42015
                                                   CIP

Printed in the United States of America.
10 9 8 7 6 5 4 3 2 1

For my mother for facing life with such grace,
and for my father for his willful determination.

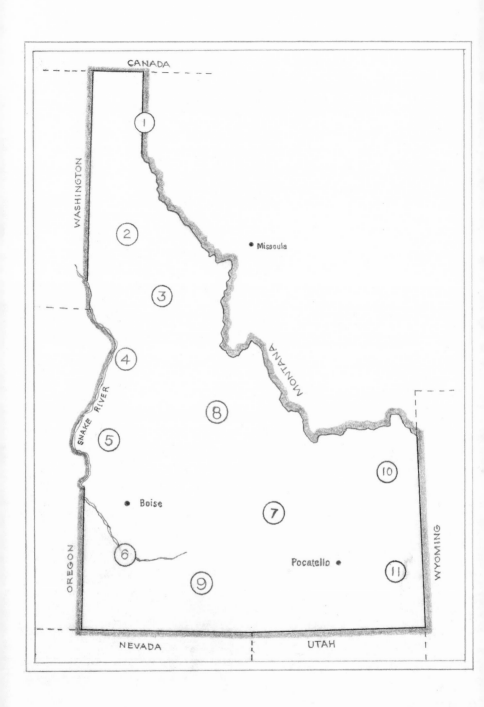

Contents

(& Key to Idaho Country Roads)

Introduction

For decades, Idahoans have joked that their state really has three capitals: the official one at Boise for the southwestern part of the state, Salt Lake City (Utah) for the central and eastern portion, and Spokane (Washington) for the Panhandle. That bit of fun and fiction does have a basis in fact.

Those three cities are the social and economic centers of their regions. They have been so since the early settlers of the Boise Valley seized the seal and papers of the original state government from the northern Idaho town of Lewiston one night in 1863, the first Mormon settlers colonized northward from Utah, and the first miners entered the Panhandle from eastern Washington.

That Idaho is forged from three distinct regions should not be a surprise, given the size of the state. At 82,677 square miles, Idaho is about as big as the United Kingdom of Great Britain and Northern Ireland. From the start of the first chapter in this book, at Cabinet Gorge Dam near the Canadian border, to the end of the last chapter, at Bear Lake in the southeastern corner of Idaho, is about 800 miles—almost the distance from New York to Chicago.

Now add to that history and size Idaho's wide variety of landforms, climates, wildlife, and vegetation. The result is a diversity of land and culture unsurpassed by any other state.

For travelers, such diversity means that a visit to Idaho can include high-desert sagebrush plains, cedar rain forests dripping with mosses and ferns, farm fields filled with the state's famous spuds, or any of 2,000 lakes or 80 mountain ranges. Idaho also offers visitors a chance to mix with loggers and cowboys, Indians from a half dozen tribal nations, desert rats and mountaintop hermits, and plenty of just plain folks, all choosing to live here because of the off-the-scale quality of life.

Idaho has a lot of wide-open space (including more acres of wilderness and more miles of wild rivers than any other state in the continental United States). With all that pristine countryside and only a million residents spread across the state, the animals have plenty of elbow-room. Visitors can see everything from eagles to elk and bass to black bears while traveling here.

My goal in writing this book has been to create an inviting introduction to this great state, my home since 1975. Researching this book, my family and I traveled more than 10,000 miles, enjoying both the opportunity to see all of Idaho and the responsibility to choose the very best routes. Each of the eleven chapters wanders through a different part of Idaho, and together the chapters provide what I hope is a compelling overview of the state.

Before beginning this journey into Idaho, you should know about a few local landmarks. Along the highways, you will see small mileposts noting each passing mile. Several times in this book, I use those milepost numbers to indicate an attraction or turn that is otherwise unmarked.

Another very useful series of signs contains the words "Sportsman's Access" above the crossed fishing rod and hunting rifle insignia of the Idaho Department of Fish and Game. The signs point to areas that are open to the public at no charge. Approximately 240 of these signs are scattered across the state. Neither a fishing rod nor a rifle is needed to use these public lands. Hikers, campers, bird-watchers, and photographers can all enjoy these places.

Introduction

All the roads mentioned in this book are two-lane paved highways unless otherwise noted. A few businesses are specifically listed in the chapters, but only if those inns, shops, or restaurants are truly exceptional and worth a visit.

I want to offer three suggestions for travelers using this book. First, take along a picnic lunch every day. There are just too many great places along streams or under junipers that you'll miss without one.

Second, try visiting the state during the "shoulder seasons" of spring and fall. Summers are warmer, everything is open, and it's certainly lovely—but during spring and autumn you'll find far fewer people on the roads and in the campgrounds. Winter means more difficult driving, but for those who love snow sports or the magnificent raw nature of the cold months, I've included wintertime information in the book as well. At all times, visitors should remember that Idaho weather is unpredictable and sometimes harsh. I'll never forget the blizzard that greeted me at Craters of the Moon National Monument in September.

Third, remember that with the state's open spaces and scattered settlements, you have to be prepared with plenty of supplies and a dependable vehicle or with a sleeping bag and an adventurous spirit. Often there are many miles between gas stations and mechanics.

For those with more questions about the state (including hunting and fishing regulations, accommodations, and outfitters and guides), the best single source is the Idaho Travel Council at 700 West State Street, Boise, ID 83720. The phone number there is 800-635-7820. The council also offers free maps and travel guides.

1 ~

Dam to Dam Across the Panhandle

From Montana (east to west): Take I-90 to Missoula, Montana, turn north on US 93 and then west on State 200 through Thompson Falls, Montana, to the Idaho border. This border crossing (the beginning of our country road tour) is 154 miles from Missoula.

From Washington (west to east): Take I-90 to Spokane, Washington, turn north on US 2 through Newport, Washington, to the Idaho border. This border crossing (the end of our country road tour) is forty-eight miles from Spokane.

Highlights: *Focus on the stunning beauty of the forested river valleys that this sixty-mile route follows, valleys that were scoured during the latest Ice Age by the world's largest flood. This country road offers a chance to sample the lumberjack's life, with visits to tiny timber towns and opportunities to see moose, eagles, osprey and their forest neighbors.*

Approaching Idaho from Montana on State 200, the first evidence of the border is the turnout on the left dominated by the billboard-size sign describing the Pend Oreille Scenic Byway. The sign lists the eleven major points of interest along the thirty-three miles of State 200 between the border and the town of Sandpoint. Corresponding signs along the road mark all of these sites, except for the Chinese cemetery at the town of Hope. Because that old cemetery is well worth a visit, you'll find those directions in this chapter.

Cruising ahead on State 200, you'll find the first must stop immediately on the left: Cabinet Gorge Dam. From the

1

viewpoint (with picnic table kindly provided), the sounds of the rushing waters of the Clark Fork River mingle with the steady hum of the turbines twirling out kilowatts of electricity.

This is an appropriate place to begin a chapter on Idaho's Panhandle, because this was the site of the Lake Missoula Flood, a cataclysmic event that reshaped North Idaho and eastern Washington. Along the Clark Fork here, between 10,000 and 20,000 years ago, huge fingers of ice moved southward from Canada, blocking the river and filling the valley with a glacial dam about 1,000 feet tall. The valley was filled with ice to the ridgetops visible from this spot north and south of the river. Water from the Clark Fork backed up behind that ice dam, creating a huge lake (known to geologists as Glacial Lake Missoula) that extended more than 100 miles into modern-day Montana.

The alternating warm and cold periods of the Ice Age caused this glacial dam to break repeatedly. Each bursting of the dam sent a wall of water downstream to the Pacific Ocean that scoured everything in its path. The bare rock outcrops visible from this spot remain as evidence of the flood's power. The two huge lakes in the Idaho Panhandle, Pend Oreille and Coeur d'Alene, were both gouged and filled by these floods. The level plain below the cities of Spokane and Coeur d'Alene—and in the Willamette Valley of Oregon—are fields of gravel and debris left by the floods. The region of rocky river courses in eastern Washington known as the Channeled Scablands also were created during the series of floods, which scientists describe as the largest floods ever recorded geologically anywhere in the world.

Since the Ice Age, the Clark Fork Valley not only has warmed considerably but also has been reforested and reinhabited by forest creatures. Continuing along State 200, you will wind through tunnels of cottonwood, birch, and evergreen trees and into open vistas of the wide river sprinkled with occasional pastures, farms, and recreational homes.

October is a great month to see the valley aflame with autumn color.

The Clark Fork moves slowly here, held to near stillness by the Albeni Falls Dam at the Idaho-Washington border more than fifty miles west, which keeps the entire water system (the Clark Fork River, which empties into Pend Oreille Lake; the lake itself; and its outlet, the Pend Oreille River) at a constant level. State 200 follows this system from dam to dam and border to border.

Today's road is built atop the traditional native pathway followed by the first white settler entering Idaho. David Thompson, a remarkable Canadian explorer and surveyor, established the first trading post in the Pacific Northwest here in 1809. That building, which he called Kullyspell House (his version of the name of the Kalispel tribe), has long since disappeared, although a historical marker along the road marks its approximate location.

Along the route, in addition to the marked attractions, you'll find plenty of unofficial picnic areas, farm and forest access roads, and roadside turnouts with paths to the river-bank. All provide a chance to explore and to find an unmarked and uninhabited piece of riverfront for hiking or picnicking.

Ahead, the first town is tiny Clark Fork. Since much of the local economy is based on cutting trees, you'll see lumber-jacks in suspenders and frayed denim pants driving huge pickups filled with wood and chain saws. The locals stop at the town's only service station to fill their tanks with gas, their cups with coffee, and their ears with the latest gossip.

At Hay's Chevron, you can expect a benchful of loggers, mill workers, and retired woodsmen trading tales. The walls of this gas station also serve as the town's "museum," hous-ing several dozen old black-and-white photos of big fish and big trees. Even if you don't need any gas, Hay's is worth a quick stop for a postcard—and a chance to sample local life.

3

Clark Fork is also the home of two fish hatcheries, each open for scheduled tours, and the University of Idaho Field Campus. The campus is a parklike refurbished U.S. Forest Service ranger station with an excellent self-guided nature trail and a small taxidermy museum, both free and open to the public. After soaking rains in the spring and fall, the forest floor along the nature trail, and even the manicured lawns of the campus, are dotted with myriad mushrooms.

On the road again after Clark Fork, you'll quickly notice that the Idaho Department of Highways was especially generous in the placement of signs along this stretch of scenic byway. Signs marking recreational sites, campgrounds, geological and historic sites, and wildlife areas dot the roadside.

Near the town of Hope, the road leaves the river valley and skirts the wide expanse of Pend Oreille Lake, named by French Canadian trappers for local tribesmen who favored decorated and dangling earlobes and now pronounced "Ponder-Ray." This lake is so deep (1,250 feet) and big (43 miles long with a shoreline of 111 miles) that the U.S. Navy used it to train submariners during World War II. Around Hope, the road passes through a cluster of private resorts, marinas, motels, and restaurants. Because of its stunningly beautiful lakeside location, this town has been a vacation destination for decades.

After passing the exits for East Hope and Hope, watch for the westernmost Hope turnoff, which will take you to the Chinese cemetery. Just past the boat basin and bridge, turn right off State 200, then immediately take the left fork, going up the gravel road past the "Local Traffic Only" sign. After driving uphill for about 100 yards, park in the small turnoff on the right, just at the start of the pavement. The cemetery is there, on the right, between the road and the dropoff to the lake. A few headstones mark the burials as turn-of-the-century. The Chinese graves are marked only with simple wooden fences. The view of the lake alone is worth the stopover. Continuing on from the cemetery through suburban Hope, you can see how generations of residents have adapted to vertical hillside living.

Beyond Hope (a bit of humor almost no one can seem to resist), you will pass my favorite sign along the scenic byway. As the road crosses the Pack River, the bold "Moose Area" sign warns visitors to watch the bottomland and the adjacent golf course for those huge creatures. If you're lucky, you'll see

Moose browse on the succulent plants found in streams and marshes and gnaw the bark from young aspens

5

one. After leaving the moose domain, the pace quickens as you enter the outskirts of the biggest city on the route, Sandpoint, population 5,000.

Just before the official city starts, on the left overlooking Sand Creek, is a visitors center and chamber of commerce office filled with brochures, maps, and knowledgeable staff ready to answer questions. Sandpoint has been treating its visitors well for many years. The first travelers information center opened here in the 1960s. After three decades of courting visitors, the town offers plenty of enjoyable shops and attractions—enough to keep travelers wandering the downtown streets for a day or more.

In Sandpoint, you'll find galleries and specialty shops, antique stores and lakeside inns, a wide sandy beach, two good museums, and an impressive selection of restaurants offering everything from family-style fare to gourmet dining. At the nearby ski resort, summer passengers as well as winter snowlovers can ride to the mountaintops in style. Anglers might enjoy searching for trophy-size lake trout. Local businesses offer visitors a chance to see herb processing, glassblowing, and cheesemaking and an opportunity to take some of the products home. The remarkable log architecture of the Cedar Street Bridge Market is a pleasure. And to tie it all together, a horse-drawn trolley runs downtown during the summer months.

Even though our country road heads west (along US 2 to the Washington border), you should turn south on US 95 for a two-mile side trip. At the southern edge of town, adjacent to yet another visitors center, US 95 crosses the Pend Oreille River on the Long Bridge. For two long miles, you drive across open water, enjoying sailboats and water-skiers, as well as osprey and views of the surrounding peaks.

The bridge is actually two parallel bridges, the new bridge for cars and the old bridge for pedestrians and bicyclists. The smooth, flat nonmotorized bridge is a mecca for joggers and cyclists. After walking or driving across the river, return to Sandpoint, following the intricate pattern of one-way streets downtown to US 2 west.

This road parallels the railroad tracks into Washington and soon leaves the commercial zone behind. The drive starts to look more inviting and more like what you left behind in Hope and Clark Fork. Again tiny towns—this time with names like Dover and Laclede—are separated by farmland, pastures, and forests. Again note the rocky hillsides, often sparsely covered with trees, that show evidence of the Ice Age floodwaters.

Another similarity with the State 200 section of this country road is an official designation. While the road from Montana to Sandpoint is called a scenic byway, the highway from Sandpoint to Washington is the official access to the Albeni Falls Dam/Pend Oreille River Recreation Area. The U.S. Army Corps of Engineers finished the dam in 1955 and then focused on developing a series of camping, boating, and swimming facilities along the thirty miles of river accessed by US 2. The result is a series of six well-maintained campgrounds, complete with sandy beaches and boat ramps, that are open from May to September. Signs along the highway point to the campgrounds, so they are all easy to find.

As you drive along US 2 near Laclede, note the small sign on the right-hand side of the road: "River Birch Farm." The sign points not to a farm but to the finest accommodations on this section of roadway. River Birch Farm is a riverside bed and breakfast, a mill owner's home built in 1903 that accepts guests by reservation only. The inn is easily missed by highway travelers but regularly filled by those who know of its charms.

Laclede, another town so small it can hardly claim existence, was built near Seneacqwuoteen, an ancient river crossing and tribal encampment. Later, beginning in the 1860s, white trappers, surveyors, and miners forded the river here on their way from "civilization" in Walla Walla, Washington, to the Kootenai gold strikes in Canada.

The only real population center in this area is Priest River, a community of 1,500 with an attractive old brick downtown off the highway to the left and a quickly developing commercial strip along the highway. There are no Big Macs here yet, but plenty of shiny new stores and eateries catering to travelers.

This town labels itself a "progressive timber community." That title, or one like it, is often applied to North Idaho towns that have noticed their traditional economic base (a seemingly inexhaustible supply of big trees employing a steady number of loggers and mill workers) getting a little rickety. Advanced mechanization, in both harvesting and milling, has drastically cut the number of jobs in the industry. Fluctuations in prices have created boom-and-bust cycles of unemployment. And the trees are no longer available in the same size or abundance.

In towns like Priest River, the recognition that the natural resource base of the local economy is unreliable has created the fear that their collective bleak future could include a downward spiral of mill closures, job losses, rapid depopulation, school consolidations, and eventually a string of empty ghost towns. That is a realistic fear in the West, where thousands of thriving communities have ceased to exist when the trees were all cut, the mines played out, or the small farms consolidated into huge agribusinesses.

The response to that threat, especially during the severe recession of the early 1980s, was the quest for economic development and diversification. Without turning their backs on the traditional resource base, towns like Priest River have sought to add other income sources, such as tourist dollars, to their economic pie. They have spruced up their buildings, encouraged local businesses that serve travelers or make finished products from local resources (creating what are often called "value-added" products), and call themselves progressive timber communities.

An interesting example of a local business based on a value-added product is just up the road in the woodlands north of Priest River. In the middle of town, turn onto State 57, the road to Priest Lake, North Idaho's most beautiful big lake. A mile past the intersection, stop at the six-sided log building on the left. That is the home of Huckleberry Creek, a business built on the delicious wild berry that grows in profusion in hillside meadows across the Panhandle.

Lora Poirier had been selling huckleberry pies to local restaurants for a decade when her husband, Kerry, lost his job in 1989. With nothing to lose, they decided to go into huckleberry products full-time. They started with a roadside table and by the summer of 1992 were able to build the attractive hexagonal store on State 57. They now process at least 400 gallons of berries annually into pies, jams, and syrups—a perfect example of adding value to a local resource and creating a viable business from the product.

Since you've begun a side trip on State 57, don't miss the opportunity to visit the Falls Inn, a half dozen miles ahead on the left. This is a typical backwoods loggers' bar, complete with the usual decor: antlers, beer posters adorned with semi-naked women, a pool table, photographs of the good old days, and a woodstove made from an old barrel. Entering the tavern is a little like stepping onto a movie set.

There are three major differences between the Falls Inn and most lumberjack bars. First, it is safe. It is known as a friendly bar, where the people who enjoy picking fights and growling at strangers don't go. I spoke at length with several unescorted women who regularly meet here to relax with their female friends. They agreed that it is indeed a friendly neighborhood tavern, a place where the locals get together to celebrate birthdays and anniversaries.

Second, it is a good place to eat. The sandwiches are huge and inexpensive. For the daring, it's a chance to sample unusual treats, such as pickled turkey gizzards.

Third, Torrelle Falls crashes twenty feet down its rocky canyon just outside the window behind the bar, then flows through a channel under the building. Patrons enjoy watching the falls, which are illuminated at night, from the comfort of the tavern. In sum, a visit to the Falls Inn is a rare chance to see Idaho backwoods culture at its most relaxed and amiable. The falls, the locals, and the beer make this spot as essentially North Idaho as anyplace you can find.

If you want more Idaho woods and water, continue ahead on State 57 to Priest Lake and the wilderness around it. When you're ready to complete this country road journey, return south on State 57 toward the town of Priest River. Another enjoyable stop along this route is Brown's Buffalo Ranch, home of sixty of the big beasts, retail buffalo products, and a pettable buffalo named Buckwheat. When you make it back to Priest River, turn west on US 2 toward the Washington border and Albeni Falls Dam six miles away.

Like virtually all Corps of Engineers facilities, this dam has a visitors center and offers tours of the power plant. After the water of the Pend Oreille River leaves this dam, it joins the mighty Columbia River, passing through fourteen more dams before it reaches the Pacific Ocean.

That's the end of this double-dam tour, a country road across Idaho's Panhandle from one border to the other.

In the Area

Clark Fork

Hay's Chevron: 208-266-9943

University of Idaho Field Campus: 208-266-1452

Cabinet Gorge Fish Hatchery: 208-266-1431

Clark Fork Fish Hatchery: 208-266-1141

Sandpoint

Chamber of Commerce (includes Hope): 208-263-2161

U.S. Forest Service: 208-263-5111

Cedar Street Bridge Market: 208-263-0502

Pend Oreille Cheese Company: 208-263-2030

Hawn-Smith Glassblowers' Workshop: 208-263-8069

Peaceable Kingdom Herbs: 208-263-8038

Schweitzer Ski Mountain Resort: 208-263-9555

Tour Boat: 208-263-4598

Vintage Wheel Museum: 208-263-7173

Bonner County Historical Museum: 208-263-2344

Laclede

River Birch Farm: 208-263-3705

Priest River

Chamber of Commerce: 208-448-1312

Albeni Falls Dam/U.S. Army Corps of Engineers:
    208-437-3133 or 208-437-5517

Huckleberry Creek: 208-448-1245

Brown's Buffalo Ranch: 208-448-2320

Falls Inn: 208-448-1046

2 ~

Into the North Idaho Woods

From Coeur d'Alene: Take US 95 south for thirty-six miles to Plummer.

From Boise: Take State 55 north for 120 miles to New Meadows, then continue north on US 95 for 230 miles to Plummer. Or leave I-84 near Payette (thirty miles west of Boise), traveling north on US 95 for 330 miles to Plummer.

Highlights: *From the heart of the Coeur d'Alene Nation, where the grainfields mingle with the forested hills, this country road heads east into the North Idaho woods for some active outdoor fun. Along this seventy-five-mile route from Plummer to Elk River, you'll have a chance to harvest wild rice in the marshes of Heyburn State Park, dig Idaho Star Garnets, find 15-million-year-old fossils, and visit the biggest tree in North America east of the Cascade Range.*

Plummer is a tiny town at the junction of US 95, Idaho's primary north-south highway, and State 5, our country road east into the Idaho timberland. In addition to the lumber mill and smattering of surrounding agriculture, the main reason for the town's existence is the Coeur d'Alene Nation.

The tribe's original territory included about 4 million acres from present-day Spokane into Montana. Through a series of treaties and reservation allotments, that area has dwindled to 345,000 acres. Due to homesteading and land purchases, only 58,000 acres within the reservation boundaries are now in Indian ownership. Most of that tribal land is located around Plummer, and the headquarters offices are a few miles west of town.

The history of the Schee-chu-umsh people is an interesting one. They were named Coeur d'Alene (meaning "heart of the awl" and now pronounced "Cordle-Ain") by French trappers who found that they were shrewd bargainers and no-nonsense negotiators who had hearts as sharp and hard as the needlelike awls they used for sewing.

One of the old chiefs had a vision of the coming of black-robed strangers who were to be the tribe's new leaders. So when Jesuit missionary Pierre De Smet arrived and, in 1842, founded the settlement and church that still bears his name about fifteen miles south of Plummer, most of the tribe was easily converted to the ways of the black-robed priests. With the death of about half the tribe from smallpox over the next few decades, the conversion was complete, and the pointy-hearted became more malleable.

Today, with mingling through business partnerships, marriage, and friendships, the tribe and their more recent neighbors have an easygoing relationship. Plummer is a great place to watch people and enjoy their diversity—from the wide, dark faces of the full-blooded Coeur d'Alenes to the lighter skin of the descendants of white homesteaders. One of the best places to people-watch is the Benewah Market, the town's supermarket and sit-down deli. The market is owned by the tribe and is housed in a larger mall building that incorporates Indian designs architecturally.

If you would rather browse than sit, try a visit to one of the other shops in the mall, the Mullen Trading Lodge. This shop has been open for a decade, under several different names, but has always focused on Native American arts and crafts. More tribal arts are usually on display at the Coeur d'Alene Tribal Headquarters.

Tribal members on the reservation are exempt from some federal tax and sales requirements. Thus, the tribe can offer high-stakes bingo at their new hall north of town, and members can sell some heavily taxed items at reduced prices. Stores owned by tribal members offer cut-rate cigarettes in Plummer and St. Maries, farther along our route. Before the Fourth of July, plywood shacks pop up like makeshift mushrooms around Plummer offering fireworks for sale.

Tribal income and federal grants have created another interesting phenomenon near Plummer—tribal housing. With the goal of bringing their people back to the reservation, the Coeur d'Alenes have built housing developments around Plummer, De Smet, and several other reservation communities. These mini-suburbs (there's one on the hill in the southeast corner of Plummer) look much like other areas of town with one exception: the fences, trees, and bushes marking property lines and privacy are missing. As one resident explained, the neighborhood is more like one big family, with all the residents related by marriage or tribal ancestry. In these family neighborhoods, everyone wants to know what everyone else is doing—and not putting up fences or other screenings makes that easy.

This country road journey is most enjoyable during the summer, May through September or October. Because it is not a well-known tourist route, there are few travelers even then. Early spring and late fall can be wet or snowy.

Heading east on State 5, you enter the domain of the "stump farmer." The first settlers of this region arrived in waves from the late 1800s through the Depression as tribal and government land was made available for homesteading. They found only forests, since the grasslands to the south and west were already claimed. Their first job was to clear the land for planting. Taking out the tree stumps was a chore best left until the wood had softened with age and the demands of building a home and barn were met. Grain was planted around the stumps, giving these homesteaders the stump-farming label. Right around Plummer, those stumps are now

14

gone, but on any side trip up into the hills you'll see the newly cleared land of modern stump farmers. This part of North Idaho has a relatively high percentage of private land, and much of it has been divided into small (five- to fifty-acre) parcels and sold to generation after generation of pioneers who still arrive ready to clear the forest.

A half dozen miles down State 5, the road enters Heyburn State Park, 8,000 acres of forest and fresh water along the southern edge of Coeur d'Alene Lake. This park is very enticing, offering more than enough reasons to spend a few hours—or a few days—hiking the trails (the Indian Cliffs Trail is especially wonderful), swimming (the sandy beach at Rocky Point is the best), boating (all 25,000 acres of lake are open to boating and waterskiing), fishing (for lake trout, bass, or kokanee salmon), or camping (the park has several large lakeside campgrounds).

Heyburn is a beautiful park, and this country road journey is a sentimental favorite of mine. State 5 was our introduction to North Idaho when we first drove to our twenty forested acres near St. Maries in 1975. I'll never forget how magnificent the lakeside cottonwoods appeared and how excited I was to be able to live in a place that looked like a three-dimensional postcard of the great Northwest.

The photo opportunities are especially tempting at the turnout a mile past Rocky Point on the left. The double band of trees that snakes into the middle of Coeur d'Alene Lake is the famed "River Between the Lakes," the shadowy St. Joe. The cottonwoods on both banks of the St. Joe River remained when the lake level was raised by the Post Falls Dam in 1911, creating this unusual sight. The banks, which have become a series of narrow islands, are wonderful for boat-in picnics.

This is the quiet end of Coeur d'Alene Lake, well away from the fast pace at the northern end of the lake. One rustic resort, the Benewah Resort, located on the eastern edge of Heyburn State Park, typifies this relaxed atmosphere with its small cabins, sunset dining room, and gently listing boat docks.

Adjacent to those docks, by late summer, more than one hundred acres of tall grass grows to six feet above the water. These aquatic grasses are North America's only commercially harvested native grain, wild rice.

Wild rice was transplanted to Idaho fifty years ago by local duck hunters eager to provide forage for their feathered targets. By good fortune, the grains brought here from Minnesota produced large kernels of the finest gourmet quality and adapted well to their new home. Reseeding itself vigorously, the rice was soon threatening to smother the Benewah Resort's docks and launching ramp.

In 1982, Heyburn State Park offered to sell harvest rights to the rice on contract, and St. Maries Wild Rice, Inc., was born. The company won that first contract and has been harvesting the rice from the park and leased farmland ever since. This small, locally owned enterprise also processes the rice for retail and wholesale delivery at its plant near the town of St. Maries, a half dozen miles ahead on State 5. The company is a success story in the area's effort to diversify the local economy away from total reliance on timber.

Bruce Peterson and Greg Runyan, owners of St. Maries Wild Rice, offer free tours of the processing plant, and even of the rice fields, when they're not too busy. Watching the fields being harvested during September is especially entertaining, as the airboat harvesters skim through the grain like huge demented water bugs. The docks, cabins, and campground at the Benewah Resort offer a close-up view of the action. Even better is a visit to the rice fields (in anything from an inner tube to a rowboat rented from the resort). Since the fields are on state land, visitors can harvest wild rice for their own consumption at no charge—just cruise through the tall stalks, bend them into your boat, and shake the ripe grains loose.

Leaving Heyburn State Park, our country road soon bisects the town of St. Maries (pronounced "Saint Mary's"), a logging community with a population of almost 3,000 and the seat of Benewah County. The town is not as spectacular as its setting at the confluence of the St. Joe and St. Maries Rivers, although Aqua Park, the riverfront park complete with several hundred yards of beach, dock, and picnic area, is a great stopover on a summer day. The Historical Hughes House museum and visitors center is the best place to begin a tour of the town.

Those interested in exploring some of the thousands of acres of backcountry around the town can find out about hiking, camping, fishing, and hunting opportunities at the local U.S. Forest Service office in the federal building downtown. Remember that the North Idaho woods are benign and inviting, with plenty of delicious wild berries to brighten summertime excursions and an absence of poisonous snakes and plants that can ruin a pleasant afternoon hike in more southerly climates.

Our country road continues southeast of St. Maries on State 3, following the St. Maries River past pastures and grainfields cleared of forest and unplowed fields that are again refilling with trees.

After climbing over a ridge a dozen miles south of town, the highway returns to parallel the river at the old town site of Mashburn, now just a railroad siding and riverside pasture. Just before the railroad bridge at the bottom of the grade, a gravel turnoff on the right ends in a small parking area adjacent to the railroad tracks and river.

That parking lot offers travelers entrance to the Canyon of the St. Maries, fifteen miles of free-flowing river downstream from this point. Hikers can follow the tracks to beautiful riverside picnic sites, and rafters can portage their gear to the river for wild springtime rides. White-water enthusiasts

17

White-water enthusiasts enjoy the St. Maries River

should understand that the river here is rocky and shallow, even during spring runoff. In addition, springtime here in the mountains can mean sudden weather changes. I have never been as cold in my life as the time we rafted this river in a warm April rain that quickly turned to snow.

Ahead on State 3, the road forks, with State 6 leading southwest back to US 95. Continue on State 3, left at the fork, through the tiny settlement of Santa. The post office and a cluster of homes are all that remain of this once-sizable logging community. For anyone interested in old-fashioned Christmas cheer, this post office is noteworthy. Postmaster Bill Rogers, along with his wife and numerous friends, are holiday elves who for decades have personally answered the hundreds of letters addressed annually to Santa Claus at Santa, Idaho.

Continuing on the country road, you'll cruise through Fernwood, the biggest town in this Upriver region and on to the home of Idaho's official state gemstone: the Idaho Star Garnet. Four miles past Fernwood, turn right at the well-marked intersection with Forest Road 447, a gravel road to the garnet fields. This area, the Emerald Creek drainage, is one of two areas in the world where star garnets are found (the other is in India).

Garnets are relatively common semiprecious purple gemstones that appear naturally as complete twelve-sided crystals up to two inches in diameter or as broken crystal chips. Star garnets are more valuable and more attractive than regular garnets due to the pointed star of four or six arms that seems to float on the surface of the polished stones when they are exposed to direct light. The star effect (known as asterism) is the result of small needles of titanium dioxide trapped within the garnet crystal. If the needles are oriented in two directions, a four-ray star results. A three-way orientation causes a six-ray star. Polished four-rays retail for about twenty-five dollars a carat and six-rays for more than twice that amount. At Emerald Creek, you can dig these stones yourself. Approximately one in ten to twenty raw gemstones is star garnet.

On the right, just off State 3, is the Emerald Creek Garnet Milling Company, a large warehouse and mill. The company digs and processes garnet sand for sale worldwide as an abrasive. With huge draglines and backhoes, workers scrape the garnet-bearing dirt and gravel from several nearby creek beds and haul it to the mill for processing.

We're aiming for the more elusive garnets—the ones residing in their native habitat—down Forest Road 447. When the road forks in four miles, bear left, continuing past the U.S. Forest Service's Emerald Creek Campground to the digging area, also managed by the Forest Service and open daily during the summer, from Memorial Day to Labor Day. The charge is four dollars per person per day, payable to the employees on duty at the office at the end of the half-mile trail from the parking lot.

You'll need shovels, buckets, work clothes, and wood-framed screens for sifting—because you'll be digging down to bedrock to find garnets mixed with the soil, roots, and rocks in the creek. It is wet and difficult work, but rewarding for those who brave the elements. The Forest Service estimates that the average garnet hound takes home a pound of raw stones per digging day.

The shoveling, sorting, and washing while up to your ankles in a cold mountain stream test the limits of fun, but I have enjoyed the thrill of a rock hound in the next puddle who has pulled out a golf ball–size, perfectly formed garnet just begging for display. The beautiful, clear purple stones with that mystical star drifting just below the surface are not only stunning set in jewelry but also precious for the tale of their discovery.

Garnets safely stowed, the next adventure awaits you down State 3—digging 15 million years into the past. A half dozen miles beyond the Emerald Creek turnoff, past the U.S. Forest Service's Clarkia office (a good place to stop for information on nearby campgrounds and outdoor activities) and through a series of riverside meadows splashed with wildflower color during the summer, watch for the Buzzard's Roost Trophy Company on the right. It's adjacent to a sign announcing the address "85th and Plum."

Of course, there is no such address. In the middle of this empty country, there is no Plum Street, much less eighty-five cross streets. The address is a bit of Kienbaum humor. As Francis Kienbaum, owner of both the trophy company and the adjacent motorcycle raceway, explains, "Well, we're eighty-five miles from Spokane and plum in the middle of nowhere."

Kienbaum made a remarkable discovery when clearing the land for the racetrack in 1971. Using his bulldozer to form the turns, he plowed through a section of dark and gooey clay. Several days later, he noticed a few leaves blowing in the wind—leaves unlike any now found in the pine and fir forests of North Idaho. The leaves (from magnolias, avocados, redwoods, and other warm-weather trees) were deposited in the fine silts of Miocene Lake Clarkia approximately 15 million years ago. The leaves were so well preserved that when Kienbaum plowed open the hillside, the leaves—the original, actual leaf structures—separated from the rock.

Geologists from the nearby University of Idaho quickly recognized that Kienbaum had unearthed a world-class fossil bed, likely the finest place to find preserved leaves from the Miocene era anywhere.

The Kienbaums live here, between the trophy company and the raceway. They have opened that fossil-filled hillside to digging for a daily charge of five dollars per person. (They also rent no-hookup campsites in the raceway parking lot.) The Kienbaums will gladly take visitors to the hill and demonstrate the digging technique.

The hillside rock is finely layered, moist, and tan-colored. The first step is to chop out a block of rock with a shovel or Pulaski. Then, turning the layers vertically, just jab at the line between layers with a dull knife (a butter knife is fine). When the knife enters the soft rock, twist to pop the layers apart. The glory of this fossil site is the abundance of perfectly preserved leaves. Almost every twist reveals a leaf on one rock face or the other. I've also found acorns, twigs, seeds, insect wings, and small branches.

I have even seen (no poetic license here, this actually occurred) leaves so well preserved that their autumn colors, reds and golds, were still clearly visible when the rock layers popped open. Unfortunately, the color of such leaves disappears in less than a minute, as the 15-million-year-old leaves rapidly oxidize to dull brown. Equally amazing, the actual leaf tissue can often be lifted off the rock. Scientists from around the world have come to the Kienbaums' raceway to find samples to test for minute changes in structure or DNA over time.

The fossil-finding equipment required is minimal. Besides the shovel and knife, all you need is a bucket or box to store the treasures and a pile of newspapers to wrap them in. Each fossil should be individually wrapped and then kept in a cool place (a basement is ideal) for several months. If you follow this procedure, they will dry slowly and not crack. Once dry, the fossils can be openly displayed. My only other hint is to time your visit to arrive on a weekday, since the racetrack is often full of motorbikes on weekends.

Digging for fossils is much less work than searching for garnets, so you should have energy left to take the free tour of the Kienbaums' trophy company. They started making trophies in 1975 to offer as prizes for their raceway winners. The Kienbaums are masters of machinery renovation. Their antique woodworking equipment—huge planers, lathes, and drills—was scrounged from junk piles and barns. All they ask for their tours is a phone call ahead, if possible, to let them know you're coming.

State 3 continues on for another fifteen miles to the town of Bovill. On the way to this tiny lumberjack community, the road rises gently out of the meadows along the upper reaches of the St. Maries River and then over the forested divide to the headwaters of the Potlatch River. As you descend the slight incline toward Bovill, the countryside returns to riverside meadow ringed with forestland. At Bovill, State 3 turns right, aiming west back to civilization. Our country road tour continues on State 8 to Elk River and the heart of the North Idaho woods.

The twenty miles of State 8 from Bovill to Elk River (where the highway and the pavement end) parallel the abandoned rail lines of the Chicago, Milwaukee, St. Paul and Pacific Railroad. The railroad line, which is still obvious along the road, was the way in for supplies and lumberjacks and the way out for lumber from the mill at Elk River during the early years of this century. The timberland here has been cut ("harvested" is the term preferred by logging companies now much more interested in public relations) repeatedly over the past century and has become just a shadow of the majestic forest that originally covered these hills.

Elk River is one of North Idaho's timberland towns that refuses to die. With the lumber mill and school gone now, this formerly bustling town is surviving on tourism and retirement. Houses are cheap, and retirees who like small-town life and the outdoor opportunities available are moving in. Backwoods guides, hotels, taverns, and restaurants dependent on travel dollars have replaced timber industry services in Elk River.

Travelers come to Elk River because there's so much to do in the miles of national forest surrounding the town and on the lake and streams nearby. The tallest waterfall system in North Idaho (Elk Creek Falls) is a few miles south of town. Sportsmen like the opportunities for big-game hunting in the unpopulated forestland and the fishing at Elk River Pond. The Morris Creek Cedar Grove provides excellent hiking opportunities. Gravel roads snake out from Elk River in all directions, providing access for sight-seeing and picnicking. Camping is permitted anywhere away from fragile creeks. (The practice of allowing "dispersed" camping away from established campgrounds is common in these unpopulated woodlands.)

In addition to all its other outdoor attractions, Elk River has the Big Tree. This 3,000-year-old western red cedar—the largest tree of any species in North America east of the Cascade Range—is located in a fern-filled valley ten miles north of town.

The Big Tree was discovered in 1979 by two U.S. Forest Service surveyors. It is more than eighteen feet in diameter and over fifteen stories tall. A tiny stream flows below and through its base, and other large cedars surround the giant at a respectable distance.

A visit to the Big Tree begins with a ten-mile drive on good gravel roads north from Elk River. Park at the gate where a wheelchair-accessible trail leads right to the tree, 100 yards ahead.

This cedar may not overwhelm those who regularly see the huge redwoods and Douglas firs of the Pacific Coast, but for Idahoans and others not used to mammoth trees, it is awe inspiring. I spent a glorious afternoon in its shadow—hiking, picnicking on the ferns, hugging the huge trunk, and sliding around its base watching the stream flow through the roots—when I discovered its existence a few years after the surveyors first found it.

The best way to learn about the location of the Big Tree—or any of the outdoor sites around Elk River—is to ask directions downtown at Huckleberry Heaven, the largest grocery store, lodge, guide service, and equipment rental shop in town. Andre Molsee, the former superintendent of schools who is the main reason for Elk River's transistion to travelers' mecca, is the co-owner of that business. While you're trying a scoop of huckleberry ice cream (made, of course, from the delicious wild berries that are quickly becoming North Idaho's trademark), ask about the Big Tree and other destinations. Molsee is quick to tell visitors about Elk River's great backyard and all that they can do during a visit.

Perhaps you'll stay in the North Idaho woods for just a few hours, but more likely the variety of attractions and the beauty of the country will keep you overnight in one of Molsee's lodge rooms (a chance for a hot-tub soak and an all-you-can-eat lumberjack meal may be irresistible). After a long journey down this country road to the heart North Idaho's timberland, Elk River is a great place to regroup, relax, and reminisce.

In the Area

Plummer

Coeur d'Alene Tribal Headquarters: 208-274-3101

Benewah Market: 208-686-1216

Mullen Trading Lodge: 208-686-1728

Heyburn State Park: 208-686-1308

Visitor Information: 208-686-1641

St. Maries

Benewah Resort: 208-245-3288

St. Maries Wild Rice, Inc.: 208-245-5835

Chamber of Commerce/Historical Hughes House:
    208-245-3563

U.S. Forest Service, St. Maries Ranger District: 208-245-2531

Upriver

Emerald Creek Garnet Milling Company: 208-245-2096

U.S. Forest Service, Clarkia Work Center: 208-245-2514

Fossil Bowl/Buzzard's Roost Trophy Company: 208-245-3608

Elk River

Huckleberry Heaven: 208-826-3405

Community Center/Visitor Information: 208-826-3209

3 ~

Montana

to Moscow

From Montana (east to west):
Take I-90 to Missoula, Montana, then go south on US 12 for fifty miles to the Idaho border at Lolo Pass.

From Moscow (west to east):
From I-90 at Coeur d'Alene, go south on US 95 for ninety miles to Moscow. From I-84 at Boise, take US 55, then US 95 north for 300 miles to Moscow.

Highlights: *Beginning at the crest of the Bitterroot Range, on the Montana border, this route follows the Lochsa and Clearwater Rivers, where the forest extends down to the water's edge, then wanders through the rolling grainfield country known as the Palouse to end at the Washington border in Moscow. The total distance is 190 miles, a journey that can be completed in a day or stretched out over a week or more.*

US 12, from the Montana border at Lolo Pass across Idaho, parallels one of the original trails across the mountains used by the Nez Perce to get to the buffalo-hunting grounds from their homeland to the west. In 1805, the Lewis and Clark Expedition also chose this traditional route, which follows the ridge north of the Lochsa River and US 12, to cross the mountain wilderness to the Pacific Ocean. During the summer of 1877, Nez Perce bands fleeing the U.S. Army after the Battle of White Bird Canyon followed this path, which was designated the Nez Perce National Historic Trail in 1986.

Virtually the entire US 12 portion of this tour (the modern equivalent of the ancient ridgetop trail it parallels) is within a national forest. An abundance of public land has kept private development to a minimum, rivers flowing freely, and forestland along the river corridor uncut and beautiful. In sum, it is a vacationer's dream, a chance to see something of what this part of Idaho was like for early visitors and inhabitants. It's also a well-traveled route regularly used by trucks hauling Montana grain to the Snake River barges at Lewiston, so drive with care.

After crossing 5,233-foot Lolo Pass (and losing one hour by jumping from the mountain time zone to the Pacific time zone), you will see the U.S. Forest Service's Lolo Pass Visitor Center immediately on your left. The center is open during the summer months for travelers and during the winter for snow enthusiasts.

As you continue on US 12 after the visitors center, the twists of the road will reveal breathtaking views of the peaks in the central Idaho wilderness straight ahead. The road descends quickly and ten miles later (at milepost 165) flattens along Crooked Fork Creek at the Bernard De Voto Memorial Grove. The road bisects a beautiful grove of western red cedar trees, named in honor of the author, historian, and conservationist who often camped here and whose ashes were scattered here following his death in 1955. Stone stairs and gravel paths are provided for those wise enough to leave their vehicles for a walk among the four-foot-diameter cedars.

At the water's edge, look in the small pools and riffles for fish. There are plenty of big ones (up to two feet long), thanks to the designation of these waters as a special management area in 1977. Anglers can fish in Crooked Fork Creek and the Lochsa River downstream to Boulder Creek, but only using single barbless hooks without bait. The catch-and-release policy here has saved the local population of native Westslope cutthroat trout (Idaho's state fish).

Ahead at milepost 162, a side road leads to the U.S. Forest Service's Powell Ranger District office, another source of information about local fishing, hunting, camping, and hiking. Next to the ranger station is the last outpost of civilization for sixty-four miles, the Lochsa Lodge. The lodge offers the last chance to load up on gasoline and groceries, or to sleep in a cabin or motel bed, until the next town. The dining room is classic Idaho mountain lodge, with trophy heads of local animal species mounted on the log walls and a great outside deck. Roadside signs warn that there is nothing commercial for the next sixty-four miles, so be prepared.

Be prepared as well for a fantastic drive along the Lochsa River. This river has a well-deserved reputation for raging rapids, with dozens of major white-water sections revered by rafting enthusiasts around the world. Along the Lochsa, plenty of riverside pullouts offer handy places to view the rapids and the thrill seekers who challenge the river in kayaks and rafts. The Lochsa is officially designated a Wild and Scenic River, and it is both.

There's also plenty of wild land around. Across the river from US 12 is the largest wilderness complex in the continental United States: the 3-million-acre Selway-Bitterroot and Frank Church River of No Return Wilderness Areas. Since no gas-powered vehicles are allowed on the south side of the river, the occasional bridges along this section are wide enough only for foot traffic and pack animals headed to the extensive wilderness trail system maintained by the U.S. Forest Service. On the north (highway) side of the river, several dirt forest roads lead uphill to sections of the Lolo Motorway, a road built upon the trail used by both the Nez Perce and the Lewis and Clark Expedition. The Lolo Motorway (Forest Road 500) is rough and dusty or muddy (depending on the season), passable only by those who are stout of heart and sturdy of vehicle. Anyone considering the route (which offers some incredible views as well as the satisfaction of traveling in the footsteps of the first visitors to this area) should check with local U.S. Forest Service officials about road conditions.

Ahead at milepost 151 is the busiest bridge (and the most popular parking area) on the Lochsa, the gateway to the Warm Springs Trail. This one-mile-long trail leads to Jerry Johnson Hot Springs, a well-known destination for Missoula students and others who like to soak in a natural hot pool.

Perhaps the best stopover along this route is at Colgate Licks, at milepost 148. This is a natural seep of warm (106°F) water laden with the carbonate salts loved by deer, elk, and moose. From the parking lot, a great trail, two-thirds mile in length, winds up an easy incline to a mountain meadow where the only sounds are from birds, the river, and the wind. The licks is in the center of the meadow, surrounded by hundreds of hoofprints. Visitors in early morning or late afternoon are most likely to see animals coming to drink. Around the licks is a scattering of big trees that share the meadow with the skeletons of dozens of cedar trees burned by a series of wildfires and felled by the wind. Because cedar is resistant to decay, these trunks will rest in this meadow for decades, adding a surreal accent to the scene.

Another source of visitor information, as well as displays of forest ranger memorabilia and on-site commentary from Forest Service retirees, is the next U.S. Forest Service site along the route, the Lochsa Historic Ranger Station, at milepost 121. After that, the next stop is Lowell, population 23, with the first commercial supplies and accommodations since the Lochsa Lodge.

Lowell is at "three rivers," where the raging Lochsa River meets the more placid Selway River to form the Middle Fork of the Clearwater River, which continues downstream along US 12. Crossing the bridge at the confluence begins a

29

twenty-mile side trip to Selway Falls. At the far side of that bridge, on the left, is the Three Rivers Resort, which functions as a mini–tourist information center, with offices for all five local white-water guides on the premises. The resort also provides riverside cabins, camping space, gasoline, groceries, river-view dining on the second-floor deck, and a bed and breakfast getaway cabin.

A paved roadway (Forest Road 223) continues beyond the bridge and past the lodge along the Selway River. Five miles ahead are the beautiful old buildings (and more local information) of the U.S. Forest Service's Fenn Ranger Station. After two miles more, the pavement disappears and the road narrows to a gravel track hugging the riverbank—a great way to see the river canyon up close. For thirteen miles more, the Selway winds calmly between cedars up to three feet in diameter.

All that changes at Selway Falls, a series of powerful white-water dropoffs that really churn in spring and early summer. Nearby is a U.S. Forest Service pack station that serves as a jumping-off point for the adjacent Selway-Bitterroot Wilderness Area. The road ends soon after the falls, forcing the choice of a return trip to US 12 at Lowell or a wilderness backpacking trip. My favorite hike in this region, among the cedars along Meadow Creek, begins at the trail-head five miles beyond Selway Falls.

To rejoin our country road tour, retrace your path to US 12 and turn left (west) onto the highway. As the route continues downstream, the pristine Lochsa corridor slowly gives way to encroaching civilization. Occasional cable trams and bridges cross the river to private homesteads, and pastures and houses mingle with forestland on both sides of the highway, as the canyon widens and flattens.

Hummingbird Haven, at milepost 84, is the home and bird sanctuary owned by Don and Ruth McCombs. Since the late 1960s, when they set out their first hummingbird feeder,

*The name of the Selway River comes from a Nez Perce word
meaning "good canoeing"*

the McCombs have hosted about 500 visitors annually. These visiting bird fanciers are drawn by the chance to sit in the shade of the McCombs' back porch and arbor and observe dozens of hummingbirds feeding and resting. I was fascinated by the abundance of the tiny creatures. They are a joy to watch, hovering and chirping, with their exquisite colors. Visitors are welcome at no charge, although Ruth suggests calling ahead to make sure they are home. The hummingbirds spend the summer on the river, from mid-April to August.

Four miles before the next town of Kooskia appears across the river, US 12 enters the Nez Perce Reservation, and eight miles along is the spiritual center of Nez Perce culture. On the left, three miles before Kamiah, is the first of several dozen sites that comprise the Nez Perce National Historical Park. This first site is called Heart of the Monster. According to Nez Perce legend, here, at the great boulder surrounded by a grassy riverside meadow, is where Coyote killed the Monster and the blood from the Monster's heart (which hardened into rock) became the Ne-Me-Poo, the Nez Perce people. In addition to visiting the interpretive center, you can picnic under the trees or walk to the river and get a sense of the reverence with which the Nez Perce view this beautiful land.

Kamiah, a lovely riverside community of 1,200, is a pleasant resting place with a host of motels, RV parks, and bed and breakfasts. You may stroll among the shops downtown or enjoy the large town park down at the water's edge. For the next twenty miles to Orofino, US 12 follows the aptly named Clearwater River.

A side trip at Greer, fifteen miles past Kamiah, leads visitors steeply uphill on State 11. Pierce, the gold-strike town founded in 1860, and Weippe, where the Nez Perce saved the Lewis and Clark Expedition from starvation in 1805, are on State 11. At Greer, The Dusty Trunk, a tiny antique store in the back bedroom of the home of Bill and Ruth Bird, is a cozy stop where visitors are as likely to share coffee and cookies as to buy antiques. From Greer, Orofino is seven miles ahead on US 12.

At Orofino, US 12 continues along the river and arrives at Lewiston, on the Washington-Idaho border, forty-two miles later. Our more scenic route leaves US 12, crossing the Clearwater into the town of Orofino and turning left just after the bridge, following State 7 toward Ahsahka and Dworshak Dam.

This new road seems to suffer from some kind of identity crisis. As it climbs out of the canyon through the grainfields above, the road changes its name four times, from State 7 to Clearwater County Road P1 to Nez Perce County Road 215 to Latah County Road P1. Throughout the journey, however, it remains a paved two-laner (though a popular one during harvest season—so watch for trucks laden with grain in late summer).

Ahsahka is the next town along State 7. It is not much more than a collection of anglers' river access sites and the home of the world's largest hatchery for steelhead, the big oceangoing rainbow trout. This hatchery is open for free tours daily, as is the visitors center at nearby Dworshak Dam, three miles ahead.

Beyond Dworshak, the highway climbs the canyon wall past patches of roadside blackberries and great canyon view of the farmland above. As the road flattens on top, you enter one of the richest grain-producing areas in the United States. Rich soil plus abundant year-round moisture equals high yields here. Wheat is king, alternated with barley and lentils or green peas. A welcome recent addition is rapeseed, grown for its oil, which blooms bright yellow in May and June.

The magnificent views from the high open fields around the tiny settlements of Cavendish and Southwick—coupled with the lack of traffic and commercial interruption—make this area a personal favorite. The road seems to flow organically around the grainfield-covered hills and up the forested draws. It's a calm and pleasant ride among farmsteads scattered across the prairie.

The road soon leaves the farms, winding quickly downhill to the valley of the Potlatch River and the town of Kendrick. This road (now named Latah County Road P1) ends at State 3 after crossing the river. Directly ahead is a massive wall of basalt columns swirling as if they were still molten. This black rock flowed from fissures in the earth in more than 100 separate eruptions during the Miocene, 6 million to 17 million years ago. Most of the Inland Northwest is covered with layer after layer of this rock. Occasionally, when the proper cooling conditions were present, the basalt hardened into columns. Where rivers or road cuts carved away the soil, the basalt layers are visible. This road cut at the end of Latah County Road P1 is the most extravagent display of columnar basalt in the area.

At State 3, turn left through Kendrick and its inviting Main Street lined with old brick buildings and locust trees that bloom in profusion in late May. On the other side of Kendrick, take State 99 out of the river canyon to the town of Troy, then turn left on State 8 to Moscow.

The hills around Troy and Moscow are steeper than those around Cavendish and Southwick, producing an unusual dimpled landscape and a unique geographic region known as the Palouse (pronounced "Pah-loose" and named for the ancient village of the Palouse tribe at the confluence of the Palouse and Snake Rivers). The Palouse hills are shaped like sand dunes, steepest on the northeast side with a long gradual slope to the southwest, because they were built by years of windblown silt and ash arriving on the prevalent southwest winds.

The Palouse is a native grassland, sandwiched between the Idaho forests and the central Washington desert, where the first explorers noted with surprise that the rich soil pro-

*The Palouse is a major grain-producing area in Idaho and
Washington*

duced grass as tall as a horse's belly. Now the same soil and
climate are producing grain on farms a thousand acres or
more in size. The steep hillsides are harvested mechanically
with self-leveling combines that are intriguing to watch.

Moscow is the largest town on Idaho's side of the Palouse
(with 18,000 residents) and surprisingly cosmopolitan in com-
position and outlook. (Moscow also is my hometown, and
boosterish pride may be coloring this description.) The University of Idaho adds racial and cultural accents to the town's

solid Idaho friendliness, resulting in a European-style downtown area with lots of unique shops and summertime sidewalk dining.

The best day to visit Moscow during May through October is Saturday. The Moscow Farmer's Market, filling a parking lot and street downtown, draws sellers of homegrown fruits and vegetables from a hundred-mile radius, artisans of all kinds, and shoppers from all around the Palouse. The trading begins by 8:00 A.M., and during the mid-morning hours musical entertainment is scheduled at the adjacent Friendship Square. The sidewalk tables fill up, friends gather in bunches to chat, and kids climb and tussle in the playground. It's a pleasant community scene.

Moscow is surrounded by outdoor recreational opportunities of all kinds (the U.S. Forest Service office in town is the place to go for ideas and directions). History buffs will enjoy a tour of the local historical society's museum (and the adjacent residential area), and the University of Idaho campus boasts a cluster of century-old buildings and the oldest arboretum in the West.

When you've seen it all, major highways lead north, south, and west from town. The Idaho-Washington border is Moscow's western edge. From Moscow, US 95 offers north-south access to the rest of the Idaho Panhandle, and State 8 becomes State 270 as it enters Washington and the town of Pullman.

In the Area

Lowell

Lolo Pass Visitor Center: no telephone

Lochsa Lodge: 208-942-3405

U.S. Forest Service, Powell Ranger Station: 208-942-3113

36

Three Rivers Resort: 208-926-4430

U.S. Forest Service, Fenn Ranger Station: 208-926-4258

Kamiah

Nez Perce National Historical Park: 208-843-2261
    Chamber of Commerce: 208-935-2290

Don and Ruth McCombs/Hummingbird Haven:
    208-926-4527

U.S. Forest Service, Kamiah Ranger Station: 208-935-2513

Orofino

The Dusty Trunk: 208-476-4593

Chamber of Commerce: 208-476-4335

Dworshak Dam Visitors' Center: 208-476-1255

Dworshak National Fish Hatchery: 208-476-4591

U.S. Forest Service, Clearwater National Forest Supervisor's
    Office: 208-476-4541

Kendrick

Visitor Information: 208-289-5731

Moscow

Chamber of Commerce: 208-882-1800

University of Idaho: 208-885-6111

Latah County Historical Society: 208-882-1004

U.S. Forest Service: 208-883-2301

4 ~

Meadow to Meadow

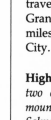

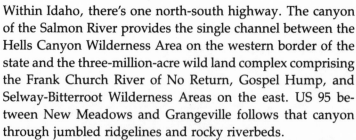

From I-84 (south to north): New Meadows is at the junction of State 55 and US 95, about 120 miles north of Boise on State 55 or 100 miles north of Payette on US 95.

From I-90 (north to south): From I-90 at Coeur d'Alene, travel south 200 miles to Grangeville on US 95, then 50 miles east on State 14 to Elk City.

Highlights: *This route links two of Idaho's most beautiful mountain valleys by following the Salmon River and then the Clearwater River from New Meadows to Elk City. The focus is on wild country, with access to several wilderness areas and abundant fish in the rivers and game on land.*

Within Idaho, there's one north-south highway. The canyon of the Salmon River provides the single channel between the Hells Canyon Wilderness Area on the western border of the state and the three-million-acre wild land complex comprising the Frank Church River of No Return, Gospel Hump, and Selway-Bitterroot Wilderness Areas on the east. US 95 between New Meadows and Grangeville follows that canyon through jumbled ridgelines and rocky riverbeds.

Our country road begins in the tiny town of New Meadows, at the junction of State 55 and US 95. The Meadows Valley is appropriately named, since this wide flat valley at

4,500 feet elevation is one huge mountain meadow, inhabited now almost entirely by cattle on huge pasturing ranches. The headwaters of the Little Salmon River flow north from this valley, and our route parallels that river (actually no more than a mountain stream here).

New Meadows is the crossroads for the northern and southern parts of this sprawling state, since all road traffic must pass through the town (resulting in a good selection of roadside diners and accommodations for a town of 600 residents). Given the area's mission as a meeting place, it is not surprising that the handful of delegates representing the scattered settlements of miners and homesteaders in the territory first assembled here in 1863. This first official meeting of a statewide political party in the brand-new Idaho Territory took place at Packer John Welch's cabin three miles east of New Meadows. A replica of that cabin is the centerpiece of Packer John State Park, a sixteen-acre campground on State 55.

Two miles north of New Meadows, on US 95, you cross the 45th parallel; halfway between the equator and the North Pole. Pull off to the right at the visitors center if you want to take a photo by the official 45th parallel road sign or pick up some brochures about the area. Across the highway is the entrance to Meadow Creek, an upscale planned residential and golfing community, and just up the road is Zim's Hot Springs, with a naturally hot swimming pool and camping facilities. For generations, Zim's has served as a handy stopover for families traveling US 95 between Boise and Lewiston. Even the most tightly wound youngsters seem to relax after a splash and soak in the hot water.

Back on US 95, you'll find more of the same glorious Idaho countryside. The meadow narrows, as the trees start to crowd toward the highway, and the calm, meadering stream accelerates into the rushing white water of the Little Salmon River. Plenty of roadside turnouts along this section give anglers and river watchers a chance to get close to the water.

At milepost 180, fifteen miles beyond Zim's, the Fall Creek Café offers good basic food served on an outdoor deck overlooking the river. Visitors also enjoy the displays inside—ranging from local historical objects to a collection of women's mirrored compacts. Another fifteen miles north, you're at the confluence of the Little Salmon and the main stem of the Salmon River, at the town of Riggins.

Riggins almost died in 1983 when the local lumber mill burned. But that same year, the seeds of its rebirth were planted. The first white-water river guide established a business in town, and now Riggins is bigger, busier, and certainly more attractive than ever. Today dozens of businesses based on recreation, not timber, form the economic basis of the town. Scores of white-water companies, restaurants, inns, and small shops line US 95 as it becomes the town's main street. Riggins is the best example of an Idaho community that has successfully made the transition from timber to tourism.

In making that transition, Riggins certainly benefited from its location on the Salmon River. The river is especially attractive to white-water enthusiasts because its entire length, including all of its tributaries, remains undammed—saved from that confinement mostly because it drains the huge central Idaho wilderness. It is the longest free-flowing river in the continental United States. There's even more romance and history in the Salmon's nickname, the River of No Return, a label given to it because the pioneers who tried to float their goods downstream would never attempt a return voyage because they knew the river was too swift and rugged.

Although the Salmon River—with all its fishing, rafting, and jet-boating potential—is the town's main draw, Riggins also serves as a gateway to the surrounding forestland and Hells Canyon. A series of dirt roads (all rough and steep) leave the river near Riggins and climb to the edge of the deepest gorge in North America (for more information on Hells Canyon and directions to another gateway to the canyon, see Chapter 5). The local office of the U.S. Forest Service for the Hells Canyon National Recreation Area and the Hells Canyon Wilderness Area is at Riggins, on the left at milepost 195.

In Riggins, with all the choices of roadside inns, you won't see signs for the best and most luxurious accommodations in the area. The Lodge at Riggins Hot Springs doesn't have a sign in Riggins because it doesn't accept guests without reservations. The lodge is nine miles from town, up the narrow paved road that hugs the bank of the Salmon River, surrounded by trees, rocks, and river. Even without any posted signs, visitors find the lodge, attracted by the quality of the site, the service, the meals, and the hot soaking pools. This ten-room inn offers the finest accommodations available in the central part of the state, from Coeur d'Alene to Sun Valley.

After Riggins, at milepost 197, as you follow the highway across the bridge, you'll leave the mountain time zone and enter the Pacific time zone. The road winds along the Salmon, with plenty of roadside pullouts offering access to the river.

Make sure to stop at the U.S. Forest Service's Slate Creek Ranger Station, at milepost 214. Slate Creek is the gateway to the southern flank of the Gospel Hump Wilderness and a must for history buffs. The Forest Service has outfitted a log cabin with old tools and housewares from the early days of the agency.

At Slate Creek, you can also get a free copy of the White Bird Battlefield Auto Tour brochure. Another ten miles ahead, at the town of White Bird, the highway leaves the Salmon River and climbs up to the Camas Prairie. White Bird is a well-known place in Idaho history (as well as the name of a Nez Perce chieftain), since it was there in June of 1877 that a band of about seventy warriors soundly defeated a much larger force of U.S. Army Cavalry in the first decisive battle of the Nez Perce War. It was a war that the Nez Perce ultimately lost, after a thousand-mile run toward freedom in Canada, but it established the tribe's reputation for horsemanship, battlefield cunning, and bravery.

Taking the auto tour will help you to visualize the battlefield and plot the opponents' strategies and positions while driving along the highway. The brochure is an excellent living history resource.

If you don't stop at Slate Creek, you can to get the auto tour brochure and others at the roadside information kiosk at White Bird. White Bird is now a tiny town at the bottom of White Bird Creek adjacent to the highway. And it is here, at White Bird, that every traveler must make the existential highway choice: old road or new. The old road is not that old; the rugged heights of White Bird Hill remained unconquered by automobiles until 1921. No road connected northern and southern Idaho until that route switchbacking up the canyon wall (the present old road) was finished.

That old highway (a paved, winding, and narrow two-laner) is longer and slower than the new express model zooming up the hill, but it is a grand tour, and one that provides the best on-site understanding of the battle. If you choose the old highway, turn off at White Bird and go uphill on the town's main (and only) street. If you select the expressway, just continue ahead on US 95, cross the bridge, and head up the hill.

Whichever route you choose, the auto tour brochure explains the half dozen stops along the road where you can see the positions taken by both forces during the battle. The two routes meet again near the crest at milepost 230, just below the last big viewpoint on the right (a great spot to enjoy the grandeur of the canyon). US 95 continues over the pass and into the Camas Prairie.

As you descend from White Bird Summit, the prairie stretches out before you, a quilt of multicolored patches, each

The records of the Bureau of Indian Affairs contain handsome portraits from the Idaho reservations taken in the 1890s, shortly after the Nez Perce War

a field of wheat, barley, or rapeseed. In the spring, isolated areas are a lush blue, filled with a multitude of camas flowers. Camas, a member of the lily family with an edible bulb that was a staple food of the Nez Perce and other inland tribes, filled the prairie before the settlers and their plows arrived, causing many early visitors to compare the entire plain to an ocean of blue. Now, only remnants are left behind.

This route, north over White Bird Hill and across the Camas Prairie, was the escape chosen by the Nez Perce in 1877. Several roadside historical sites mark skirmishes along that route, as the Nez Perce aimed for their ancient trail to Montana (there's more on the Lolo Pass trail in Chapter 3).

A few miles ahead is Grangeville, the biggest town on the Camas Prairie and the county seat of Idaho County. As US 95 approaches the town, watch for State 13, which goes right through the middle of this community of 3,500. The town offers everything a traveler needs, including a couple of distinctive shops worth a visit.

The Ray Holes Saddle Company is the oldest complete custom saddlemaking company in the United States. From its downtown shop and western goods retail store, the company sends beautiful custom saddles and horse tack by mail order around the world. Ray Holes's son Gerald Ray is now the master craftsman. Visitors can take a free guided tour of the store and shop and are then free to wander, and even to ask questions of the leather masters at work.

Martin's Antiques is a jumbled collection of nineteenth-century western gear, a museum where everything is for sale and available for close inspection. Ralph Martin specializes in Native American artifacts and crafts and in cowboy and cavalry gear. Here you can hold—and buy—a real piece of the Old West.

Ahead on State 13, at the far end of town on the left, is the U.S. Forest Service Supervisor's Office for the Nez Perce National Forest. This office is information central for camping, hunting, fishing, rafting, and hiking questions about the region. It's also the place to ask about access to the nearby wilderness areas, selecting a hunting or fishing outfitter, or hiring a white-water guide.

State 13 out of Grangeville is a white-knuckle ride for those who are squeamish. Vistas of the forested shoulders of the Clearwater River canyon and the seemingly endless ridges that almost brought the Lewis and Clark Expedition to an end open up at every turn. The route is beautiful enough to have been officially designated the Clearwater Canyon Scenic Byway.

At the bottom of the canyon, State 13 ends at State 14, and a right turn here puts you fifty miles from the end of this country road at Elk City. Note the first sign on the right—"Rough Road." Even though this is a paved two-lane Idaho highway, it is a little-used access to a virtually unpopulated piece of forest. There's no gasoline, and very few reminders of commercial civilization, available along this road. The annual freezes and thaws leave their pimply reminders in the pot-holed roadbed, and much of the route is without the customary guardrails to mar the views of the South Fork of the Clearwater River on the right. In sum, it's a great getaway.

The steep canyon walls are heavily timbered on the northern slopes, while the south-facing slopes, which bake in the summer sun, are covered with more grass than trees. Plenty of U.S. Forest Service campgrounds, official river access sites, and informal riverside trails and campsites line this road, with private homesteads only rarely interrupting the wild country. The route is too wiggly to allow you to go more than 50 mph very often. However, don't let the lack of traffic lull you into complacency; a logging truck could appear around any bend, or the overhanging rock ledge at milepost 28 could take you by surprise.

Watch the road cuts along this route. The folded layers of rock are the remainders of the inland seas that covered this part of the world one billion years ago. Those rocks were wrinkled and twisted by the force and heat of the granite rock of the Idaho Batholith, which pushed upward in the central part of this state about 100 million years ago. Besides folding that ancient rock, the batholith also brought minerals to the surface, specifically veins of precious metals that sparked the gold rush to the Elk City area in the 1860s. A group of twenty prospectors from the earlier strike at Pierce found gold in this area in May of 1861. By that fall, Elk City had forty stores, saloons, and cabins.

On our route, by milepost 36, you will see big piles of almost-bare rock that indicate previous dredging operations that separated the gold from the riverbed. At milepost 43, take Crooked River Road to the right (on the bridge over the Clearwater) to see the devastation of this earlier mining process. About fifteen miles of the entire valley floor were dredged. All the dirt and vegetation washed downstream, and the rocks were left in rippled piles. The land is slowly restoring itself, as grass, brush, and trees are beginning to cover some of the rock piles. About one-half mile from State 14, a different kind of restoration is occurring. The U.S. Army Corps of Engineers and the Idaho Department of Fish and Game built a fish-tagging facility to sample and study the recently reintroduced populations of salmon and steelhead in the Crooked River. The facility is open intermittently from February through November, and any of the biologists stationed here will give you a tour.

Because of the early wealth and population the gold strike brought, Elk City is today a surprising anomaly in terms of land ownership. The Elk City township (the thirty-six square miles around the town) and a few scattered mining claims are not owned by the U.S. Forest Service. Everything else in the entire South Fork Valley is national forest. On the map, Elk City is an island of private and state land in a sea of

Forest Service green. That explains the Bennett Company lumber mill, which is the first evidence of the town as State 14 approaches Elk City.

At the mill, the South Fork of the Clearwater River is formed by the confluence of the Red and American Rivers. The road that follows Red River to the right past the mill leads to Red River Hot Springs (with a café, rustic cabins, hot pools, and no phone on the premises—requiring guests to confirm reservations through the owner's brother's phone) and even farther to the town of Dixie. Dixie is so isolated that electricity and telephone service just arrived in the 1980s. At Dixie, travelers can find accommodations and great meals at the locally famous Lodge Pole Pine Inn.

Our country road tour follows State 14 to the left after the mill, continuing along the American River (more a creek than a river) to Elk City, two miles ahead. Before arriving at this town of 300, the road leaves the narrow river canyon and suddenly enters an area very similar to the Meadows Valley at the beginning of the tour. Both are wide, open grassy valleys located high in the mountains (Elk City is at 4,200 feet elevation, while New Meadows sits at 4,500 feet). The towns that form the valley's population core are almost equal in size, and both valleys are filled with large hay and cattle operations. Both also are ringed with high mountains that mean picture-postcard views from almost anywhere nearby.

The big difference between the two areas is the road-ways. New Meadows is bisected by busy US 95; Elk City is literally at the end of the road. Little-used State 14 stops in the middle of Elk City, spreading its minimal traffic to a series of gravel forest roads. Whereas there's always something moving at New Meadows, quiet is a way of life at Elk City—except during hunting season.

Because of Elk City's location in the center of miles and miles of prime forest habitat, the town fills up during the fall with pickups, trailers, and bearded men wearing plaid shirts and camouflage hats. Autumn visitors who don't like hunting should keep that opinion to themselves.

To accommodate the overflow hunting crowds, Elk City has plenty of taverns, restaurants, and inns. The best place to find out about these services—and, of course, anything related to camping, hiking, hunting, or fishing—is at the U.S. Forest Service's Elk City Ranger Station, conveniently located in the middle of town. The rangers here also can direct really adventurous drivers to the Magruder Road—the long dirt road to Montana that forms the border between (and the only wheeled access to the midpoints of) the state's two huge blocks of wild land, the Selway-Bitterroot Wilderness Area and the Frank Church River of No Return Wilderness Area.

The only tavern in town that's not in the middle of town, right on the highway, is Trapper's. Well-known Elk City barkeeps Vee and Trapper Bettencourt operate a saloon in their basement. It's much more inviting than the average basement bar, since their 5,000-square-foot house sits atop a hill on the edge of town and the big airy basement offers great views of the valley and the surrounding mountains. Trapper looks the mountain man part, and listening to his stories of life at the end of the highway—and watching the snow melt off the top of Iron Mountain from his deck—is an appropriate way to end this journey from meadow to meadow.

In the Area

New Meadows

Packer John State Park: 208-634-2164

Chamber of Commerce: 208-347-2322

U.S. Forest Service, New Meadows Ranger Station, 208-347-2141

Meadow Creek: 208-347-2555

Zim's Hot Springs: 208-347-9447

Riggins

Fall Creek Café: 208-628-3838

U.S. Forest Service, Hells Canyon Ranger Station:
208-628-2916

Chamber of Commerce: 208-628-3778

The Lodge at Riggins Hot Springs: 208-628-3785

Rapid River National Fish Hatchery: 208-628-3277

Slate Creek

U.S. Forest Service, Slate Creek Ranger Station:
208-839-2211

Grangeville

U.S. Forest Service, Nez Perce National Forest Supervisor's
Office: 208-983-1950

Chamber of Commerce: 208-983-0460

Nez Perce National Historical Park: 208-843-2261

Ray Holes Saddle Company: 208-983-1460

Martin's Antiques: 208-983-1340

Elk City

U.S. Forest Service, Elk City Ranger Station: 208-842-2245

Trapper's Tavern: 208-842-2547

Dixie

U.S. Forest Service, Red River Ranger District: 208-842-2225

Red River Hot Springs: 208-983-2800

Lodge Pole Pine Inn: 208-842-2343

5 ~

Going to

Hell

From I-84 (south to north): Begin at the intersection of I-84 and US 95 about fifty miles west of Boise.

From I-84 (north to south): From I-84 at Baker City, Oregon, go east on Oregon State 86 for seventy miles to Oxbow, then continue north for twenty miles to Hells Canyon Dam on Forest Road 454.

Highlights: *Beginning in the fertile cropland valleys of the Snake, Payette, and Weiser Rivers, this route descends into hell by following the Snake River north to the end of the road, the entrance to Hells Canyon. This ninety-mile route could be a day trip into the deepest canyon in North America, but all visitors should be forewarned. That canyon is more a paradise than a vision of Hades. The beauty of the canyon and the available camping areas may be enough reason to extend a visit to a week.*

From its junction with I-84, US 95 winds north through Fruitland, Payette, and Weiser. All three communities, especially Weiser, have well-preserved downtowns located off US 95 that will excite fans of local history and small-town values. These communities were all founded in the late nineteenth century as agricultural centers, supplying the local farmers who dug canals to use the abundant water of the Snake, Payette, and Weiser Rivers to make the desert soil yield more than sagebrush and tumbleweeds. Although the wide, flat valleys are green now with a variety of orchard and field crops, the dry and treeless hills attest to the area's true climate.

Weiser, about twenty miles north of the interstate, has managed to achieve a modest fame with its annual National Oldtime Fiddlers' Contest. During the third week of June, thousands of visitors from across North America fill this city of 4,500 to overflowing. Impromptu jam sessions and informal competitions erupt spontaneously in every park and camping area, in addition to the official competitions and the established marketplaces for musical mementos.

The Weiser Chamber of Commerce office downtown is adjacent to the National Fiddlers' Hall of Fame—a required stop for anyone who gets remotely excited by that type of music. The chamber office also can supply brochures for self-guided tours of the town's historical buildings. Even if you don't take the tour, at least walk a few doors east of the office to the Pythian Castle, a turreted sandstone wonder built in 1904 by the Knights of Pythias. The castle is totally out of place in this otherwise staid downtown and the best architectural fantasy in the state.

Equally interesting is the Intermountain Cultural Center and Museum west of town. In 1899, Rev. E. A. Paddock established the Intermountain Institute on this site to offer a high school education to boys and girls who lived in remote areas. Each child attended classes and then worked five hours a day at the institute. After educating more than 2,000 students, the Intermountain Institute was closed by the Depression. The building was used to house the town's public high school until Weiser High School opened in 1967. Now it is the home of the county museum and a gift shop, and remains a beautiful building, with a clock tower that can be seen for miles around.

North of Weiser on US 95, the cropland quickly surrenders to the encroaching desert, as the road climbs Midvale Hill. At the crest, 3,326 feet in elevation and fifteen miles from Weiser, take the turnout to the left at the Midvale Hill Rest Area for a stunning view of the central Idaho mountain ranges to the north. The tallest peaks on the left are the Seven Devils, the mountain range to the east of Hells Canyon. Our country road will take us first in front of, and then to the left (or west) of, that range and into the depths of the canyon.

Continue ahead another dozen miles on US 95 to Cambridge (population 400). This is a collection of well-kept homes and attractive storefronts in the midst of cattle-grazing country. One business here deserves special notice. Kay's Cafe is where the locals eat. The work boots and spurs on these loggers and ranch hands are real, and the wall of napkin art is an ode to undiscovered genius.

Cambridge is the last major outpost before Hells Canyon. Here our route leaves US 95 to follow State 71 west, descending to the deepest gorge in North America. This river canyon was so treacherous for either water or land transportation that early travelers saw it as a vision of hell.

Today State 71 provides, in sixty-two paved miles from Cambridge to Hells Canyon Dam, easy access to the same rugged canyon. As the highway leaves Cambridge along Pine Creek, it follows the same route used by herds of sheep until the 1950s. The animals wintered in the canyon, spent the summers in the mountain meadows in the center of the state, and used this route to move between the two locations.

Three dams block the Snake River ahead. Brownlee, completed in 1959, is the first. This dam created a fifty-seven-mile long reservoir that stretches back to Weiser. You'll actually cross this dam into Oregon for ten miles until you reach the next bridge downstream at Oxbow Dam. Oxbow Dam was completed in 1961. Hells Canyon Dam, twenty miles ahead, was erected in 1968. A fourth dam planned for farther downstream would have flooded Hells Canyon and changed the Snake River there from a series of rapids into placid reservoir. The passage of the Hells Canyon National Recreation Area

Act in 1976 eliminated the option of building more dams in the canyon and preserved forever the majestic beauty of this 8,000-foot-deep gorge.

The three dams that turned the upper section of Hells Canyon into stair-step ponds had an undeniably positive impact on the region. Together the dams generate about a million kilowatts of electricity annually and have created plenty of jobs, both in their construction and in their continued operation. The reservoirs provide their own boating and fishing recreation, and downstream areas are better protected against flooding.

However, there has been a negative effect. Thousands of acres of riverside farmland and wildlife habitat were inundated. Towns and archaeological sites were eliminated. The salmon and steelhead that had returned annually to the tributaries of the upper Snake River were made extinct. Also, because the sand coming downriver is trapped by the dams, beaches and spawning habitat below the dams have been destroyed.

Together these three dams have created ninety-five miles of slack water. Anglers praise this development, since prime habitat for bass (both smallmouth and largemouth), crappies, rainbow trout, and catfish was established so that the ocean-going salmon and steelhead could be replaced. Another benefit of these impoundments are the beautiful campgrounds built by the utility that constructed the dams, Idaho Power Company.

Idaho Power maintains four campgrounds along our route, offering showers, rest rooms, and hookups at reasonable prices (four dollars for tent sites, six dollars for RV sites). Reservations are not accepted for any of them, and there are no on-site caretakers. The only way to find out about availability and local river conditions is to call Idaho Power's toll-free number and listen to the recorded message.

This road along the reservoirs provides a hint of the majesty of the canyon ahead, with steep and rocky walls reaching down to the water's edge. The only settlements are the company towns that house utility employees and a scattering of small private campgrounds. The best place to get Hells Canyon information along this route is at the office of Hells Canyon Adventures, a river outfitter that offers both jet-boat and raft trips through the canyon. (Jet boats are aluminum-hulled craft powered not by propellers but by jet pumps, enabling them to roar through even the rapids in the canyon.) The office is located eight miles past Oxbow Dam.

Most visitors to Hells Canyon begin their journey at the bottom (or downstream) end of the canyon in Lewiston, 100 miles north of Hells Canyon Dam. Lewiston is the best source for Hells Canyon information. The Chamber of Commerce office there even has a toll-free number. In addition to supplying maps for those interested in road or trail access to the canyon, chamber officials can provide lists of outfitters that carry visitors into the canyon by raft or jet boat.

Our route ends at Hells Canyon Dam. The Snake River rushes downstream from this dam, crashing and twisting over rocks that form some of the most exciting white water in Idaho. Access into the canyon from here is by water (a boat ramp is provided below the dam) or by foot. The Snake is relatively calm for a half dozen miles below the dam, and propeller boats can enter the water with care for fishing or sight-seeing. A series of massive rapids follows and no prop boat should try to navigate these waters.

Exercising extreme caution in the canyon is advisable. But to anyone who comes to Hells Canyon Dam, that warning is unnecessary. Upon first look, this canyon looks hellish. There is nothing to indicate that people are welcome. The canyon walls are very steep and rise skyward without a break. The river roars with real teeth that can easily ravage any boat.

I stood with awe for several minutes at my first view from this dam, wondering how I could ever force myself into a raft that challenged such a mighty river. Once in that raft, however, I had the ride of a lifetime, including a visit to the Green Room, a twenty-foot-deep hole in the river where our raft went vertically down, stabilized for a millisecond, and then was pushed upward again by the surging greenish water.

The twenty-mile stretch below the dam forms the heart of the canyon, offering the most exciting white water anywhere. The Hells Canyon Wilderness Area lines both sides of

These pack trains are en route to Hells Canyon for a camping trip

the river in this section. Downstream, outfitters' cabins and even some private homes are scattered on the shores as the river flattens in its approach to Lewiston.

A visit to Hells Canyon is a heavenly experience. This canyon supported hundreds of families through the Depression. The homesteaders carved small, flat garden spaces up the side canyons, and, with the warm climate and abundant water coming from the mountains above, they grew plenty of food. Fish (bass, salmon, steelhead, and the huge freshwater sturgeon) and deer, mountain sheep, and other game provided all their protein needs. A hike up any side canyon today will reveal the remnants of their orchards and gardens, including grapevines, apple trees, and plum trees that are still productive today.

Part of this canyon's beauty is its isolation. You really have to want to get there to be there. Another part of the attraction is its stark magnificence. The rocks are sharp and rise upward like skyscrapers. If you're standing at the river, the mountain peaks—more than a mile almost directly above—are clearly visible. No place in Idaho is as humbling as Hells Canyon.

In the Area

Fruitland
Chamber of Commerce: 208-452-4350

Payette
Chamber of Commerce: 208-642-2362

Weiser
Chamber of Commerce: 208-549-0452
Intermountain Cultural Center and Museum: 208-549-0205

Cambridge

Visitor Information, Inland Power Company: 208-257-3815

Kay's Cafe: 208-257-3561

Hells Canyon

Lewiston Chamber of Commerce: 208-743-3531 or
  800-473-3543

Hells Canyon Adventures: 503-785-3352 or 800-422-3568

Idaho Power Company: 800-422-3143

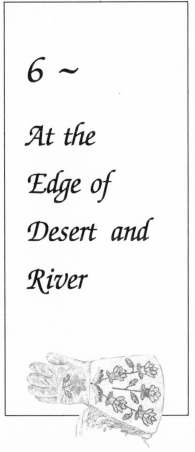

6 ~

At the Edge of Desert and River

From Marsing (west to east):
The town of Marsing is about fifteen miles west of the Boise metropolitan area and two miles east of US 95. Begin at the intersection of State 55 and State 78 in Marsing and continue southeast on State 78 for eighty miles to Bruneau Dunes State Park.

From Bruneau (east to west):
Bruneau Dunes State Park is near the intersection of State 51 and State 78, eighteen miles south of I-84 at the Mountain Home exit. Begin at the park and continue west for eighty miles on State 78 to Marsing.

Highlights: *State 78 follows the border between Idaho's driest desert, the Owyhee, and the state's biggest recreational river, the Snake. A century ago, this route was part of the Oregon Trail, a section dreaded by pioneer travelers because of its desolation. This is still rough country, hot in summer and cold in winter, but filled with beauty, and home to few people.*

This country road from Marsing to Bruneau is entirely within Owyhee County, a county about as big as the state of New Jersey but with a population of approximately one person per square mile. Most of the county's 8,300 residents live at the ends of State 78, clustered around Marsing and Homedale on the west and Grand View and Bruneau on the east. Virtually all of the county's 7,600 square miles are unpopulated desert. The northern border of the county is the Snake River.

Visitors may find this rough country most hospitable during the spring and fall. Avoiding the climatic extremes of winter and summer results in more comfortable cruising.

The county's name comes came from a local spelling and pronunciation of Hawaii, which is one of the places in the world least like the desert in Idaho's southwest corner. The desert, the county, and the river that crosses them both were named for three Hawaiian fur trappers who joined David McKenzie's expedition in 1819. The three were sent exploring up the rivers into the desert. When they never returned, McKenzie investigated, discovering one murdered and two missing. Wanting to honor the three, but not being too certain of the spelling of their home, McKenzie settled on the current name. It sounds almost the same as Hawaii, if you say it fast enough.

Marsing is a small agricultural community, dependent on irrigating the desert. The town does boast a remarkable restaurant, the Sandbar Riverhouse, famed for its dining on a deck overlooking the river. Other than that, there's not much in Marsing. Make sure to stock up on gasoline and other provisions here, as miles of inhospitable desert stretch ahead.

Irrigation holds the desert at bay for a few miles past Marsing, but soon you'll see only the same rocks and scrub that frightened the Oregon Trail pioneers. The Snake River on the left is an elongated oasis, a thin green-and-blue stripe in the midst of the dryness. To the right, the mountains baked nearly bare are the Owyhees. Expect some excellent views of the stark desert landscape along this route.

If you're ready for a restful stop, pull over at milepost 11, at Givens Hot Springs. Travelers have indulged in restful soaks in this heated mineral water for millennia. White visitors learned of its refreshing powers from the local Indian tribes, and it became a well-known stopover on the Oregon Trail. In 1881, the Givens family opened a hotel here, and the present campground, pools, and cabins are operated by their descendants. Besides the big indoor pool (kept at 96°F in summer and 99°F in winter), three small private tubs (where

Travelers on the Oregon Trail stopped at Givens Hot Springs for a soak

you can control the temperature up to 118°F) are available. Busloads of schoolchildren visit the pool regularly, so call ahead if you're hoping for a quiet soak.

Ten miles past Givens Hot Springs, State 45 leaves State 78 and crosses the Snake, heading toward Boise. Past this bridge, the bluffs on the far side of the river grow taller and steeper. The combination of ready food sources (fish in the river and desert-dwelling rodents) and ideal nesting habitat has made this region world famous as raptor country. Hawks, falcons, eagles, and owls by the hundreds live on those basalt cliffs. Almost half a million acres of cliff and desert along eighty-one miles of river have been protected as the Snake River Birds of Prey National Conservation Area. Direct access from our country road route to the conservation area is difficult, requiring transit along a maze of dirt roads. The best choice for travelers anxious to see the raptors is to take State 45 to Boise or to complete this route and return to Boise on the interstate. Visitors should begin at the World Center for Birds of Prey just south of Boise.

After passing the State 45 intersection, State 78 leaves the river canyon and travels inland through the treeless black hills and the scrubby sagebrush plains of the Owyhee Desert. This countryside is controlled by the Bureau of Land Management of the U.S. Department of the Interior. Camping and hiking are allowed anywhere. There are no developed campgrounds, and the established trails are designed for use by off-road vehicles. The only regulations are designed to keep those vehicles on the trails to save the fragile desert environment.

In the midst of this seemingly endess desert, at milepost 29, is the Owyhee county seat, the tiny town of Murphy, population 50 and known as the smallest county seat in the United States. (Since the county has two centers of population located at its east and west borders, the residents decided to put the county seat right in the middle, so everyone would have to drive to get there.) The county courthouse is about all there is to Murphy. To celebrate the eccentricity of putting a courthouse in the middle of miles of nothing, Murphy was given a parking meter (the only one in the county) by some jokester residents. Placed right in front of the courthouse in the 1950s, surrounded by unlimited free parking, the meter was never opened until the late 1980s, when it was blasted by a vandal's gunshot. The sheriff found it stuffed with coins and tokens. The meter was replaced and remains there today, a reminder of the town's unusualness.

The Murphy International Airport serves as another reminder of Murphy's uncommon nature. Located just across the highway from the courthouse, the airport is actually, despite its big-city label, just a single paved runway and a wind sock.

The town does offer travelers the basic services (café, gasoline, convenience store, post office) and the Owyhee County Museum, located behind the courthouse. The museum is actually a complex of buildings and displays, including the Marsing train station, a caboose, the Murphy schoolhouse, and a sod-roofed, log-walled settler's cabin.

Four miles beyond Murphy, a gravel road to the right winds 23 miles and climbs 4,000 feet into the mountains to Silver City. In the 1860s, during the town's mining boom, more than 8,000 people (the same as the present population of the entire county) lived here. Now the town has two caretaker/residents in the winter and a population of about twenty in the summer. Some of Silver City's great old buildings have been maintained and restored. The Idaho Hotel still rents rooms during the summer, and a gift shop and café are open regularly. Everyone shares the same phone number, using an old-fashioned crank system. Silver City is a beautiful old town in a delightful mountain setting—but the trick is getting there.

The one road into town turns to impassable mud in the winter and is closed from November 1 through June 1. Even when it is officially open, the road is not always drivable. Visitors should check at the sheriff's office in Murphy before starting the climb to Silver City.

Back on State 78, you'll continue east through more of the same landscape to milepost 50, where some bold white lines have been drawn across the highway. This is a fake cattle guard—a real one would be made of steel bars spaced evenly apart and buried across the road—to prevent cattle from crossing. (The cattle can't differentiate between a

Gamblers and miners once cooled their heels at this now-ghostly jail in Silver City

fake guard and a real one.) This guard marks the border between the desert rangeland behind and the agricultural area ahead.

The irrigated farmland begins again, and alfalfa and row crops replace sagebrush. State 78 again parallels the river, and several riverside parks and boat ramps are marked with "Sportsman's Access" signs. The first settlement is Grand View, an aptly named farming community with a population of 330.

Just past Grand View is one of the most popular fishing and boating destinations in Idaho, the C. J. Strike Wildlife Management Area. With a total of 12,500 acres surrounding the Snake River, the area offers plenty of places to play. This wildlife management area includes boat ramps both above and below the C. J. Strike Dam, which widened the river into a reservoir. There's also plenty of parking and water access for anglers, hikers, and anyone who enjoys wildlife observation. About 100,000 ducks and geese winter here, plenty of deer, pelicans, shorebirds, pheasants, and beaver live here year-round. The park headquarters is just off State 78 on the left, two miles before the intersection of State 51.

After that intersection, continue to follow the highway (now both State 51 and State 78) east across the Bruneau River to the town of Bruneau (pronounced "BREW-no"). At the far end of this little settlement, note the intersection with Hot Springs Road. The twenty-mile side trip down this road leads to a remarkable viewpoint. The first eight miles off the road are paved, but the last twelve are gravel. As you drive across the flat desert, it's easy to forget that the road parallels the Bruneau River. But if you take the short access road to the Bruneau River Overlook, you'll never forget it again. Here the river has eaten a steep and narrow canyon through the black basalt rock that underlies the desert, and the view is breathtaking. The canyon is 1,200 feet wide and 800 feet deep.

Back on State 78/51, you'll climb out of the river valley and get a great view of the Owyhee Desert and the Owyhee Mountains. Just before the Snake River, the highways divide. State 51 continues north to the town of Mountain Home and I-84. Stay on State 78, to the right, for two miles, to the entrance to Bruneau Dunes State Park.

The focus of this 4,800-acre park is the largest single sand dune in North America. The 470-foot-tall dune and an adjacent smaller sand hill cover 600 acres in the center of a circle of desert hills known as Eagle Cove. When the Bonneville Flood (see Chapter 11) released a wall of water down the Snake River about 15,000 years ago, an eddy at Eagle Cove filled with eroded sand. Since then, the unique wind pattern here (winds blow equally often from the southeast and the northwest) has piled the sand into a dune and kept the dune moving around in the center of this natural bowl.

Whatever the geologic history, the result is a great park setting. Bruneau Dunes is a magnificent place for sand-pattern photos, desert hikes, and wildlife observation. This is also the home of one of the world's more bizarre sports, sand skiing (using old snow skis or sleds to slide down the dunes). The park includes a campground, grassy picnic area, and boat ramp for the small lake adjacent to the dunes. Especially in the heat of summer, the air-conditioned visitors center, with its great displays of everything from fossils to barbed wire, is a big draw.

At the park, visitors can hike anywhere, free to observe the lizards, hawks, and jackrabbits that make this hostile landscape their home. Climbing the sand dunes gives visitors an opportunity to see the fascinating patterns of ripples and swirls that the wind can build.

This park is the essence of the Owyhee Desert, a place where wind and dryness conspire to rob the land of all vegetation and where the most extreme desert conditions rub the earth raw, down to its basic elements.

In the Area

Marsing

Sandbar Riverhouse: 208-896-4446

Chamber of Commerce/Visitor Information: 208-896-4122

Givens Hot Springs: 208-495-2000 or 800-874-6046

World Center for Birds of Prey: 208-362-3716

Murphy

Bureau of Land Management: 208-384-3300

Owyhee County Museum: 208-495-2319

Silver City: 208-495-2520

Owyhee County Sheriff: 208-495-1154

Grand View

City Hall/Visitor Information: 208-834-2700

C. J. Strike Wildlife Management Area: 208-845-2324 or 208-465-8465

Bruneau

Bureau of Land Management Fire Guard Station: 208-845-2011

Bruneau Dunes State Park: 208-366-7919

7 ~

The Road
to Nowhere

From Mountain Home (west to east): Leave I-84 at exit 95, following US 20 east. Past Arco, 150 miles later, take State 22, skirting along the northern edge of the Idaho National Engineering Laboratory. Forty miles later, turn left onto State 28 up the desolate Birch Creek Valley to end at Gilmore, sixty miles from that intersection.

From Gilmore (east to west): Beginning at Gilmore really means beginning at the town of Salmon, which is on US 93 south from I-90 at Missoula, Montana. Gilmore is fifty miles from Salmon on State 28. Continue south from Gilmore to the first intersection (State 22) sixty miles later. Turn right (west) on State 22 and continue west on US 20 when those roads intersect forty miles later. Follow US 20 150 miles to I-84.

Highlights: *The high desert that forms the border between the central Idaho mountains and the agricultural heartland of the Snake River plain. Remarkable geologic formations (including desert cold springs, Craters of the Moon National Monument, and the Big Lost River's underground home) line this 250-mile country road. Gilmore, Idaho's greatest ghost town.*

The central Idaho mountains sag southward onto the Snake River plain. Like a belt that tucks the flatland below that chubby paunch, US 20 slides along the high-desert borderland from I-84 to Montana.

From relatively urban Mountain Home, the population density declines to zero at Gilmore. This is indeed the road to nowhere.

This is also a road that can bake in summer and freeze in winter. The long distances between provisions and assistance suggest that all visitors come prepared. The more comfortable spring and fall seasons are wise choices.

Departing from the interstate at Mountain Home, US 20 very quickly leaves the trappings of civilization behind. What's left are miles of sagebrush-covered desert, occasional turrets of dark lava rock on the treeless hills, and lines of willow trees winding through the valleys following stream-beds. A series of small lakes, held behind earthen dams, fill in the spring but sizzle away as the summer progresses. At the larger reservoirs, where water remains year-round (unless drought conditions exist), campgrounds and private resorts offer lowland residents some respite from the summer heat. Periodically, patches of green are irrigated to life in the bottomlands.

By milepost 115, where the highway enters Boise National Forest, the high-country heart of central Idaho (with plenty of camping, hunting, and fishing opportunities) can be seen to the north. Eight miles later, the road bisects Castle Rocks, a patch of beautifully weathered granite outcroppings poking upward through the black basalt lava rock that flowed around them. This area was a landmark on that section of the Oregon Trail known as Goodale's Cutoff.

The pass here is more than a mile in elevation (5,527 feet) and forms the western edge of the Camas Prairie. That valley is dotted with ranches now, instead of the blue-flowered camas lily that gave its name to both the valley and the county.

Camas County is home to about 700 people, who are easily outnumbered by the cattle and sheep that also live here. Three hundred fifty people, half of the county's population, live in Fairfield, the county seat and sole metropolitan area.

Fairfield, on US 20 sixty miles from Mountain Home, is friendly to visitors (plenty stop by on the way to Sun Valley every year). A free campground and all the necessary services are available. If for no other reason, plan a stop here to tour the caboose.

As an Idaho Centennial project in 1990, the local Camas County Civic Organization remodeled the caboose into a visitors center. Volunteers staff the center daily in the warmer months. This site offers not only brochures and local information, but also the chance to see the interior of a caboose and understand how these box-shaped cars were used by rail workers. Unfortunately, the caboose visitor center has no telephone. Phone requests should be directed to the local U.S. Forest Service office.

Continuing ahead, at the junction five miles past Fairfield, State 46 leaves US 20 for a side trip south into the desert hills. The Gooding City of Rocks—a collection of twisted towers of hardened volcanic ash surrounded by miles of sagebrush—is twenty miles down State 46. This stone city, which has been preserved by the U.S. Bureau of Land Management, is an especially good stopover for car-weary youngsters who need some energetic exploration.

Back on US 20, you'll wander east for another twenty miles to the intersection of State 75, the access road to Sun Valley and the Stanley Basin (the focus of Chapter 8). US 20 bisects a remarkable basin, where water from the mountains to the north bubbles up in springs and then collects in creeks. The result is a very rare ecosystem—a place where cold water flows through the desert. The plants that live along these cold streams are the same as those that grow along the warmer streams nearby, but the aquatic life is very different.

The constantly cold water from the springs flows through these nutrient-rich streams. The result is a world-class trout fishery made famous by author Ernest Hemingway. Anglers from around the world have made pilgrimages to this area for decades, both because the trout grow to record sizes and because they are notoriously finicky eaters. This is the place for the ultimate fishing challenge.

Cattle and sheep graze on ranches in the high country

Many of the area's cold streams are on private land or have been sucked dry for irrigation. But the premier stream, Silver Creek, has been preserved by the Nature Conservancy and is open for fishing and hiking. Silver Creek is a remarkable desert oasis and should not be missed.

To visit this magnificent site, turn right on the gravel road at milepost 183. After one mile, the road curves to the left, and you'll see the wooden fence that marks the edge of Nature Conservancy land. Continue ahead for two miles to the small log visitors center on the left by the parking lot. Silver Creek Preserve is open daily at no charge, although donations are accepted.

The Nature Conservancy protects more than 5,000 acres and 20 miles of streams here. Access is restricted to foot or nonmotorized boat. No camping or fires are allowed. A signed mile-long nature trail and dozens of other paths leave from the visitors center.

To return to the highway, continue on the gravel road beyond the visitors center. This road crosses Silver Creek at the edge of the preserve boundary next to a primitive boat launch and then returns to US 20 one mile later.

At this intersection, turn right to the tiny town of Picabo and the continuation of our route, or turn left for another fun side trip to the Idaho Department of Fish and Game's Hayspur Fish Hatchery.

Wise visitors who choose the Hayspur side trip will follow US 20 west for one-half mile to milepost 185 and the gravel road that leads to the hatchery. The hatchery is less than a mile down this road, and to get there you'll pass an open field dotted with trees and picnic tables. This is a free campground operated by the Department of Fish and Game. Also on this road is the Loving Creek Restoration Project, a section of stream that the same department has made into a trophy trout fishing area.

The gravel road ends at Hayspur, the state's oldest fish hatchery, originally opened in 1907. Free tours are offered daily, but the real crowd pleaser is the rainbow trout brood stock pond, holding the hatchery's mature fish. For a dime, you can buy a big handful of fish food. When you toss the pellets into the pond, hundreds of flashing fins will churn the water. With the sun shining into the pond and shimmering off the iridescent flanks of the big fish, it's easy to see how the rainbow trout got its name.

The fish in the brood stock pond and in other tanks at the hatchery supply about 250,000 trout eggs to Idaho hatcheries annually. This facility also raises juvenile trout for transplanting throughout the region.

A second small pond at the hatchery is reputed to be the best stocked fishing lake in the state. It is wheelchair accessible and regularly filled with plenty of rainbow trout. Besides fishing and fish watching, this hatchery is great for bird watching. Eagles winter here, and ospreys migrate through in the spring.

To return to our country road tour, backtrack down the gravel road and turn left (east) on US 20. The next town has just a few buildings, which is perhaps befitting its now-you-see-it-now-you-don't name, Picabo (pronounced "Peek-a-boo").

The highway continues its wandering way eastward along the base of the mountains for another thirty miles past Picabo. Huge flat slabs of black rock occasionally dot the sagebrush along this route. These are recent flows of lava that have oozed from cracks in the earth and then hardened like pancakes on a grill. The black rock is so recent in some cases that very little vegetation has had a chance to establish itself. The best—and most recent—examples are inside Craters of the Moon National Monument.

The eighty square miles of this monument were repeatedly covered with lava from 15,000 to 2,000 years ago. This geologic wonder is a great lesson in earth building that should not be missed.

Craters of the Moon is on US 20 at milepost 229. A seven-mile loop road accesses miles of trails that lead to caves, cinder cones, and tree trunks entombed by the molten rock. The visitors center and day-use area are open year-round, but the campground closes during the cold months. Midwinter visitors flock here for great cross-country skiing.

Twenty miles past Craters of the Moon on US 20, which merges with US 93 and US 26, is the town of Arco, made slightly famous as the first city in the world to have its electricity supplied by nuclear power. The nuclear installation responsible is the nearby Idaho National Engineering Laboratory, referred to locally as INEL. The 890 square miles of INEL (that's roughly equivalent in size to the state of Rhode Island) have been the site of various military gunnery ranges, nuclear reactors, and nuclear waste piles since the laboratory's creation in 1949. Free tours are offered.

The border of the INEL is about five miles ahead, past Arco on US 20. Just past that border, our route follows State 22 to the left at its junction with US 20.

For a quick side trip and a lesson in belowground waterways, follow US 20 toward Idaho Falls. Five miles later, pull into the rest area on the right. The river channel there is almost always empty because it is the Big Lost River. Except in the wettest weeks of the spring, this river disappears into the sand in this area. The water in the Big Lost River (as well as the water in Birch Creek and the Little Lost River) enters an underground channel here, only to reappear more than 100 miles later at Thousand Springs (see Chapter 9). This rest stop offers several "riverside" picnic tables, good geologic displays, and rest rooms.

To continue on our journey, retrace your route to the junction of State 22 and follow it eastward. While continuing on this route, notice the layers in the mountainsides to your left. Geologically, this is classic basin and range country, like most of Nevada, Utah, and the surrounding areas.

This region was once ocean, and the tilting layers you see now in these mountains were the seabed. An especially good example of these layers is at milepost 4 on State 22. These originally flat layers of rock are still grinding together and piling onto one another due to the movement of the earth's tectonic plates. These mountains, like the Tetons on the Wyoming-Idaho border, are the relatively recent result of these forces, having begun growing about 6 million years ago. The 1983 earthquake, which raised the Lost River Range about two feet (more on this in Chapter 8), is an index of this continuing process of mountain building.

The uniqueness of this region is made more obvious by turning to a map rather than viewing from the road. On any road map, notice the three parallel roadways (US 93, State 28, and the gravel road from Howe to May) that go northwest from our route. These three roads follow the valleys, or basins, between the Lost River, Lemhi, and Beaverhead mountain ranges.

These three basin-range patterns are especially clear examples of the kind of folding and lifting continuing throughout the interior western states. Continue ahead on State 22 to the easternmost of these roadways, State 28. Turn left (north) at the intersection of State 28 forty-five miles from Arco.

State 28 follows Birch Creek up the valley. For those who want to camp, fish the creek, or get a closer look at the stream, the Bureau of Land Management has provided an eight-mile-long campground. The Birch Creek Campground is primitive, consisting of rough spaces between the streamside trees, some scattered picnic tables, and a few outhouses. It is a beautiful desert oasis and a great place to stay while traveling this route. Access to the camping area is at milepost 44.

This route to Gilmore is one of Idaho's most desolate and least traveled highways. The valley is at 7,000 feet elevation, and the extremes of the seasons and dryness year-round make it difficult for anything but sagebrush and jackrabbits to thrive. The mountains framing the valley sport healthy forests, but the harsh land along the highway is colored in variations of brown, resembling the stark black-and-white photographs of Ansel Adams. Its openness and monocolored contrasts lend the region an unusual beauty.

Out here civilization consists of isolated cattle ranches and one store (however, the store, which is at Lone Pine at milepost 47 on State 28, can supply a multitude of needs, with its one gas pump, RV sites, a café/tavern, and limited groceries). The outpost at Lone Pine is the only business for fifty miles in both directions, so be prepared.

Given the lack of wood in the valley, it is bizarre to find a collection of charcoal kilns nearby. At milepost 61, a six-mile gravel road leaves the highway to wind through the desolate beauty of this desert and end at the Birch Creek Charcoal Kilns. This is a side trip well worth the time. Here the U.S. Forest Service (Targhee National Forest) has constructed a picnic area with an astounding view of the valley and the Continental Divide atop the Beaverhead Mountains on the Montana border to the east. The picnic area has a hand pump for water, some tables, and a short interpretive trail around the four adjacent kilns.

The kilns were built in 1886 to supply an efficient fuel—charcoal—for the Viola lead and silver mine across the valley. For three years (until the ore ran out), each beehive-shaped brick oven was regularly loaded with thirty-five cords of wood cut from the hillsides above. After a controlled smoldering of the wood, nine tons of charcoal were removed and hauled to the mine's smelter. Approximately 300 laborers cut wood and made charcoal here. A small town, named Woodland, was built near the kilns, though no evidence of it remains.

The twenty-foot-tall kilns are made of orange brick, and their color sets them brightly apart from the tawny desert that surrounds them. You can stand inside these huge ovens and smell the pungent odor of turpentine that has lingered there in the brick for more than a century. After sampling the sights and smells, return down the gravel road to State 28.

As this country road continues north toward Gilmore, note as evidence of the isolation of this region the seventy-mile-long Lemhi Range to the left (west). This is the longest range in Idaho uncrossed by any road. Also watch carefully for antelope bounding through the sagebrush. This is prime habitat for these elusive creatures.

At milepost 73, a large historical marker on the right tells the tale of the town of Gilmore. A gravel road leads to the left (west) to what's left of that settlement and then continues five miles farther on to Meadow Lake Campground maintained by the U.S. Forest Service (Salmon National Forest).

Gilmore is the collection of buildings clearly visible from the highway. In the 1920s, thanks to several nearby mines, Gilmore was a town of 500. From 1903 to 1929, this was the second richest lead- and silver-producing district in Idaho (after the incredibly rich Coeur d'Alene Mining District), with production valued at more than eleven million dollars. But that boom busted, and gradually everyone left. The ghost town that remains is Idaho's best. Although it is on private land, the town site and its buildings are open to visitors. Nothing may be taken from the site, however.

The two dozen buildings left standing all show evidence of the rich heritage of the mines. The homes and commercial buildings have hardwood floors, wallpaper, and cement steps and foundations. This is not a collection of shacks.

This is the nowhere we've been aiming for on our journey along Idaho's high-desert midline. Gilmore is silent, except when the wind swirls through the trees or slams a cupboard door. And that's a fitting end to this country road journey.

In the Area

Mountain Home

Chamber of Commerce: 208-587-4334

U.S. Forest Service, Boise National Forest: 208-364-4100

Fairfield

U.S. Forest Service, Fairfield Ranger Station: 208-764-2202

Visitor Information/Camas County Civic Organization:
P.O. Box 337, Fairfield, ID 83327

Bureau of Land Management, Shoshone District Office:
208-886-2206

Picabo

Silver Creek Preserve: 208-788-2203

Hayspur Fish Hatchery: 208-788-2847

Arco

Craters of the Moon National Monument: 208-527-3257

Idaho National Engineering Laboratory: 208-526-0050

Chamber of Commerce: 208-527-8287

Gilmore

Bureau of Land Management, Idaho Falls District Office:
208-524-7500

U.S. Forest Service, Targhee National Forest: 208-523-3278

U.S. Forest Service, Salmon National Forest: 208-756-2215

8 ~

The

Diamond

in the

Heart of

Idaho

From Stanley (from the west):
Follow State 21 east for 120 miles
from I-84 near Boise to Stanley,
then travel this country road loop
on State 75 either east toward
Challis or south toward Ketchum.

From Ketchum (from the south):
Follow US 93 north for twenty
miles from I-84 at Twin Falls to
the intersection with State 75.
Continue north on State 75 for
sixty miles to Ketchum. Travel
this loop route either north on
State 75 to Stanley or east on Trail
Creek Road toward Mackay.

From Challis (from the north):
Follow US 93 south for 210 miles
from I-90 at Missoula, Montana,
to Challis. Travel this loop either
south on US 93 toward Mackay or
west on State 75 toward Stanley.

Highlights: *The Stanley Basin and
the surrounding White Cloud Mountains and Sawtooth Range. The
incredible beauty of this area, now
preserved by the Sawtooth National
Recreation Area and surrounding
national forest, makes for an easily
accessible vacation spot. Four road-
ways in the region connect to form a
diamond-shaped route almost 200
miles long.*

There is a diamond in the heart of Idaho. Four connecting
roads create a diamond-shaped loop through the Stanley
Basin region, a high-elevation area of incredible beauty.
Beginning at the town of Stanley and moving south, visitors
on this loop route travel sixty-one miles through the basin,
then up over Galena Summit to Ketchum. The next side of the
diamond leaves Ketchum on Trail Creek Road, headed east
for forty-one miles to US 93 in the valley of the Big Lost River.
To follow the third side of the diamond, head north on US 93
for thirty-seven miles to the intersection with State 75 near

Challis. To complete the loop, follow the Salmon River for fifty-five miles on State 75 back to Stanley.

This diamond drive is almost 200 miles, a tour through magnificent country that deservedly has been pictured on postcards and captured in snapshots for decades. This route follows paved two-lane highways for all but the Trail Creek Road section.

Travelers must exercise extreme caution driving Trail Creek Road. It is a narrow gravel road that is generally closed by snowfall from October through May. Limited road maintenence often results in ruts, rocks in the road, and bumpy conditions. Low-slung sedans must be especially careful. Check road conditions by contacting the U.S. Forest Service Ketchum Ranger District. There are no services along Trail Creek Road and very limited services on the other segments of this loop route.

Trail Creek Road is impassable in winter, and the other sections of the diamond drive are often covered with snow or ice during that season as well. Winter driving through this high-elevation area is difficult and risky. However, because of the quality and quantity of snow, plenty of visitors choose winter travel here. At more than 6,000 feet in elevation, these towns and the mountain valley routes between them can get very cold. The Idaho record of minus 50 degrees was set at Stanley. Be prepared if you attempt winter driving along this route.

Our country road tour begins at Stanley. This tiny town (population almost 100) seems much bigger than it is, perhaps because it sprawls through a treeless part of the valley at the intersection of State 21 and State 75, or perhaps because most of the buildings offer traveler services and are filled with visitors, not residents. The town retains an element of the Old West with an abundance of log buildings, wooden sidewalks, and, of course, the spectacular views.

Around Stanley's modest commercialism, the land flows across meadowland valleys dotted with cattle, then upward to the peaks of the Sawtooth Range and White Cloud Mountains, two miles in elevation. Everywhere you look, the scene is startlingly beautiful.

Leaving Stanley, heading south on State 75 (a route now officially designated the Sawtooth Scenic Byway), you'll follow the Salmon River upstream through an area so pristine that it seems frozen in time—and indeed it is.

This entire valley, and the mountains on both sides, form the 750,000-acre Sawtooth National Recreation Area. When the recreation area was created in 1975, development effectively stopped. The U.S. Forest Service, which administers the area, bought conservation easements from the owners of the large cattle ranches that fill the basin, which eliminates property division and development. Most of the existing resorts and private businesses were allowed to remain but cannot expand significantly or destroy the aesthetics of the area.

The result is a basin that will always maintain the wide-open feel of the old West. It really gets dark here at night. The widely scattered pinpoints of light that shine from ranch windows, cabins, and campfires cannot obscure the brilliance of the Milky Way. All the stars that you forgot even existed sparkle brightly. This is a magnificently quiet, wild, and inspiring place—truly the heart of Idaho.

The highway is wide, flat, and ideal for bicycling. Plenty of visitors choose that mode of transportation. All drivers should be aware that they are sharing the road with these two-wheeled vehicles and be careful.

The U.S. Forest Service provides a free cassette tape detailing the historical and geological wonders of this Stanley-to-Ketchum route. You can pick up the tape at the Stanley Ranger Station. This ranger station, located at milepost 187 three miles south of Stanley, is worth a stop even for those who don't want a tape. The view is excellent, the log building attractive, and the information abundant and free. The tape covers the fifty miles ahead on State 75 to the recreation area headquarters near Ketchum. It should be returned at the headquarters building (a similar tape that covers the same route in reverse is available at the headquarters, to be left at the Stanley Ranger Station).

The Salmon River parallels the highway. This is the same river, the longest undammed river in the continental United States, that earned its nickname, the River of No Return, by crashing wildly to meet the Snake River near Lewiston. Here it is a calm mountain stream gliding along the flat valley floor.

The river is aptly named because salmon swim the 900 miles and 6,500 feet in elevation up the Columbia River system from the Pacific Ocean to spawn and die here at Idaho's heart. Their young, born in the cold, fresh water of this basin, float downstream and slowly adapt to salt water. In the ocean, the salmon grow to maturity. About four years later, the adult fish force themselves upstream, past all the dams and rapids, to this basin to begin that mysterious cycle again.

These salmon runs are imperiled, as the fish are unable to get past all the dams from this basin to the ocean and back again. A major recovery effort is now in place. You can learn about this effort at the Sawtooth Fish Hatchery and the U.S. Forest Service's Redfish Lake Visitors Center. The hatchery, at milepost 184, and the visitors center, at milepost 185, offer displays and brochures that tell the saga of the salmon.

Campgrounds abound in the Sawtooth National Recreation Area, mostly clustered around boat ramps at Redfish and other lakes. Thousands of miles of trails crisscross the foothills and aim toward the high country for hardy backpackers. Plenty of turnouts, picnic areas, and side roads are available for those who want to enjoy the scents and silence of the high-country air.

For those who prefer pampering, more than a dozen resorts and lodges are scattered around the Stanley Basin. The most famous is the Redfish Lodge, but the best is a few miles past that site, at milepost 180: the Idaho Rocky Mountain Ranch. The log lodge and cabins were built in the 1930s. The ranch's riverside swimming pool is heated by natural hot springs. It's a great treat to stay here or just stop by for dinner.

Continuing along this diamond drive, the highway soon leaves the valley floor, climbing steeply to the must-stop Galena Overlook at milepost 159. At a wide curve near the crest, a small facility comprising a visitors center and open courtyard overlook has been built to provide a fantastic last farewell to the mountains, river, and forests below.

After crossing the 8,701-foot Galena Summit, State 75 enters the valley of the Big Wood River. Ahead, at milepost 137, the beautiful headquarters building of the Sawtooth National Recreation Area is on the left. Soon thereafter, the highway leaves the national forest to enter the suburbs of Ketchum/Sun Valley, the most affluent spot in Idaho. This is a land of abundant wealth and palacial estates.

Across the open sagebrush-covered hills and through the stands of birch and cottonwood trees lining the rivers, you can see the trails cut across the ski mountains ahead. This region has some of the finest ski conditions anywhere. Lots of powdery snow and clear sunny days are the hallmarks of the winter here. Thanks to the money of railroad magnate Averell Harriman, the nation's first destination ski resort was established here. Several resorts now fill this small valley.

But this area is not a wintertime destination only. During the warm months, golf, hiking, fishing, and hunting are some of the outdoor activities that attract visitors.

Author Ernest Hemingway was drawn to this area for those outdoor pleasures. He killed himself at his home here in 1961 and is buried next to his fourth wife, Mary, in the Ketchum Cemetery. To visit the grave site, turn left into the

Hundreds of miles of trails through the Sawtooth Range and White Cloud Mountains encircle Idaho Rocky Mountain Ranch

cemetery, just past the golf course, at milepost 129, on the northern edge of Ketchum. The Hemingways are buried in the rear center of the cemetery, about forty feet from the back fence, in a grove of three pine trees. Each grave is covered with a horizontal slab of marble inscribed only with their names and birth and death dates. The site is as sparse as Hemingway's writing.

For both Ketchum and Sun Valley, two adjacent towns that really form one community, the warm months are the off-season. The towns are less hectic then, and the dozens of boutiques are less crowded. More than twenty miles of paved bike paths, and many more miles of trails, follow the river and climb into the hills.

At Ketchum's main intersection, this diamond drive leaves State 75 and turns left (east) on Sun Valley Road, following the signs to Sun Valley. Within a quarter mile, at the Ketchum Ranger Station on the left, this road enters Sun Valley. For those planning to continue ahead on this loop route, the ranger station is a wise stop. This is the best source of information on the condition of Trail Creek Road (as well as everything you need to know about camping or hiking along the route).

Two miles past the ranger station, you'll see a small sign at the break in the wooden fence on the right that marks the Hemingway Memorial. You don't have to be a Hemingway fan to appreciate this beautiful site. Pull off to the right in the parking lot adjacent to the biking/jogging trail, and follow the short path to the side of the canal. Below, Trail Creek splashes along the edge of a golf course, but here the canal waters run smoothly in front of a bust of Hemingway and a brass plaque with the poetic eulogy the author once wrote for a friend. This site is a fitting farewell to the Ketchum area, for now our route aims for the wild high country.

The next road sign stops all but the most intrepid travelers with a warning that is correct some of the year: "Road Closed Ahead." Two miles past the Hemingway Memorial, at the entrance to the Sawtooth National Forest, there's yet another warning: "Road Not Maintained Beyond This Point by the Idaho Transportation Department. Pavement Ends Five Miles Ahead. Next 22 Miles Unpaved."

Those who are prepared for the rough road and continue on are amply rewarded. Trail Creek Road is one of the finest drives in Idaho. It is also one of the least used (the signs do have that effect). The first nine miles wind steeply up to Trail Creek Summit, on a road first cut into the cliff to haul ore from and supplies to the local mines. The view of the Trail Creek valley is awe inspiring.

At the crest (elevation 7,896 feet), the road immediately widens and flattens, and the errant roadway rocks disappear. After those first nine miles, this is just a pleasant ride on a gravel road across a wide, high-elevation valley. Sagebrush is the dominant plant, and pines and firs take over on the hillsides surrounding this plateau. It's all federal land here—no farms or ranches, only wide-open space. Pull over anywhere to enjoy the quiet and the big views. Side roads lead to even better views, great creekside picnic spots, and a multitude of camping sites.

Trail Creek Road continues ahead through the valley of the Big Lost River (see Chapter 7 to learn where this river ends). As the road approaches US 93, the pavement returns and scattered ranches begin to appear. Cultivated fields line the river, as farmers use this fertile soil to grow hay, oats, and other cold-weather crops. At the edges of the farms, the sagebrush crowds in again. Looming ahead is the Lost River Range, which includes Borah Peak, Idaho's tallest mountain (elevation 12,662 feet). Since the view is so magnificent, it is surprising that so few people travel this road.

When Trail Creek Road dead-ends at US 93, turn left (north) toward Challis, following the third side of this diamond drive. While on US 93, watch the sagebrush plain to the right for antelope and an earthen ledge. The antelope, playful deerlike creatures that bound quickly across these flatlands during the day, are more readily spotted. Finding the earthen ledge requires more scrutiny.

In 1983, an earthquake was centered here. It split the earth in the valley, lifting the mountains (including Borah Peak) two feet and dropping the valley about five feet. The earthen ledge (it's called a scarp by geologists), where the split actually occurred, parallels US 93 about two miles to the east (or right) of the roadway. The scarp is twenty miles long, seven feet tall, and clearly visible at the base of the mountains.

The U.S. Forest Service built a simple but fascinating information center here to explain the quake and its effects. About five miles from the intersection with Trail Creek Road, turn off US 93 at Double Springs Road. The intersection is clearly marked, and it's the only road that winds up into the mountains along this part of the highway. Follow this gravel road for two miles to the information center, which is a cluster of picnic tables, outhouses, informative signs, and a fenced perimeter. The fence keeps people and animals out of that section of the scarp, minimizing erosion and preserving the raw cut of the earth.

A small stream, Willow Creek, provides a green oasis nearby for picnics. The rest of the scarp, north and south of the protective fencing, is open for exploration. You can stand in the narrow canyons, inspect the ledges that were created by the quake, and imagine the force that could alter the earth in such a dramatic way.

In 1983, I interviewed three people who were in this area hunting when the quake hit. Lawana Knox, then a forty-four-year-old sawmill owner's wife from Challis, was walking, gun in hand, when the quake threw her to the ground. She watched the earth slice open with a roar; she said it looked as if the land was being cut with a giant scissors. John Turner and Don Hendricksen, twenty-eight-year-olds from Boise out hunting in Hendricksen's four-wheel-drive truck, found themselves suddenly flying around the cab like rag dolls. Their elbows, knees, and heads did $600 worth of damage to the cab. Forty feet away, they watched as the ground dropped away. Turner said that he had never felt so insignificant as he had during that quake.

Returning to US 93 and our country road tour to Challis, you'll see the scarp for another fifteen miles slicing along the base of the Lost River Range. The 1983 quake was just the latest in a 6-million-year process of mountain building in this region. (That process is described in more detail in Chapter 7.)

When US 93 dead-ends at State 75 near Challis, turn left (west) to complete the fourth side of the diamond drive. At the intersection, visitors interested in the gold-mining history of the area should plan a stop at the Land of the Yankee Fork Interpretive Center. Several state and federal agencies cooperatively manage the Land of the Yankee Fork Historic Area, to preserve the remnants of mining history that remain along the Yankee Fork of the Salmon River.

Near the interpretive center, a gravel road winds over the mountains to the valley of the Yankee Fork. This route, now known as the Custer Motorway Adventure Road, follows an earlier toll road built to haul supplies to the mines. The side trip on the Custer Motorway is a backcountry adventure that provides a real sense of the perils experienced by early miners. It's also a very rough road not recommended for trailers, RVs, or low-slung sedans.

The town of Challis (population 1,200) is located two miles to the right. All visitors services are available here. Challis Hot Springs offers RV spaces and cabins, both with access to the natural hot water in its pool.

State 75, the final facet of the diamond loop, follows the Salmon River upstream to Stanley from the intersection with US 93. In recognition of its beauty, State 75 from Stanley to the Montana border is officially designated the Salmon River Scenic Route. Visitors to this narrow canyon, which is filled with the wild rushing waters of the Salmon River, are not disappointed.

The U.S. Forest Service provides plenty of camping and picnic areas along the road, and it's easy to find pullouts at the river's edge. River runners in rafts, kayaks, and boats challenge the white water on this section of the Salmon, and their adventures provide enjoyment for bystanders as well. (Visitors who want to try white-water boating can locate outfitters

Sunny days, terrific runs, and plenty of powder lure skiers to Sun Valley

in Challis, Salmon, or Stanley through the local chamber of commerce or ranger district.)

Forty miles from Challis, the first major intersection appears at milepost 203. On the left, a paved trail from the parking area leads to the confluence of the Yankee Fork and Salmon River. A new overlook site, with signs explaining the historical background, provides a great view of the river and the remnants of the only dam ever built on the Salmon.

In 1909, the Sunbeam Dam was constructed to supply power and water for mining. Because the dam impeded the passage of salmon into the Stanley Basin, the Idaho Department of Fish and Game blew it up in 1934. Now only part of the wall remains. The rest of the dam has become just another rapid on the river.

Across State 75 from the Sunbeam Dam Overlook Site is the tiny community of Sunbeam. Sunbeam is little more than a collection of cabins, outfitters, visitor services, a convenience store, and a remarkable gourmet restaurant. The Sunbeam Cafe is an unpretentious restaurant with a great selection of regional beers and imported cheeses that is open from May through September.

Past Sunbeam, Yankee Fork Road provides access to the mining region that prospered in the valley of the Yankee Fork at the turn of the century. This road connects, via the Custer Motorway Adventure Road, to Challis. The twelve-mile drive up Yankee Fork Road to the town of Custer is a great side trip, and one without all the hazards associated with following the entire motorway to Custer.

On the Yankee Fork Road side trip, three miles past Sunbeam and State 75, the pavement ends and the dredge piles begin. Here, from 1940 through 1952, a gold dredge the size of a five-story building ravaged the valley. The dredge scooped up the entire riverbed and spit out the rocks that remained as the dredge piles visible today, saving the gold hiding there and washing the silt down the river. Today the valley remains a moonscape of raw rock.

The dredge responsible for the destruction of the valley is at the end of the piles, another seven miles ahead. The Yankee Fork Gold Dredge Association is restoring this floating earthmover and offers tours of the machinery on board during the summer.

Two miles past the dredge is the town of Custer. The population here peaked in 1900 at 500 miners, shopkeepers, and their families. The Custer Museum, in the old schoolhouse on the left, and the Emporium, where the Friends of the Custer Museum operate a snack store directly across the road from the museum, are open from mid-June through Labor Day. An easy walk around the remains of the ghost town of Custer provides a window into the miners' world.

The road up the Yankee Fork continues on all the way to Challis, but this ends our side trip. To continue the country road tour, return to State 75 in Sunbeam and turn right toward Stanley.

Two miles from the intersection of Yankee Fork Road, plan a stop at the Sunbeam Hot Springs, at milepost 201. The U.S. Forest Service has restored a beautiful stone bathhouse built at the river's edge by the Civilian Conservation Corps in 1937. Originally, the hot water from the springs was piped into the bathhouse. Now only the shell remains, and the hot water pours directly into the Salmon River at the end of a short paved path past the bathhouse.

At the river's edge, the hot water cascades down the canyon wall to mix with the cold water of the river. Sulfurous steam rises from the tiny wading pools built by visitors to collect the water. This is the site of the "boiling fountain" first described by trappers of the Hudson's Bay Company in 1824.

Continuing on State 75, ten miles past the hot springs, the road suddenly leaves the narrow canyon and reenters the Stanley Basin. The river calms, the valley widens, and the majestic spires of the Sawtooth Range appear ahead. The diamond drive is complete.

In the Area

Stanley

Chamber of Commerce: 208-774-3411

Idaho Rocky Mountain Ranch: 208-774-3544

U.S. Forest Service, Stanley Ranger Station: 208-774-3681

U.S. Forest Service, Redfish Lake Visitors' Center: 208-774-3376

Redfish Lodge: 208-774-3536

Sawtooth Fish Hatchery: 208-774-3684

Ketchum/Sun Valley

Chamber of Commerce: 208-726-3423 or (800) 634-3347

U.S. Forest Service, Ketchum Ranger Station: 208-622-5371

Sawtooth National Recreation Area Headquarters: 208-726-7672

Mackay

U.S. Forest Service, Lost River Ranger District: 208-588-2224

Challis

U.S. Forest Service, Challis Ranger District: 208-879-4321

Bureau of Land Management, Salmon District: 208-756-5400

Land of the Yankee Fork Interpretive Center: 208-879-5244

Challis Hot Springs: 208-879-4442

Sunbeam

Sunbeam Cafe: 208-838-2260

U.S. Forest Service, Yankee Fork Ranger Station:
208-879-2201

9 ~

Beyond Bliss

From Bliss (west to east): Leave I-84 at Bliss/US 30 (exit 137) and continue on US 30 toward Twin Falls.

From Twin Falls (east to west): Leave I-84 at the Twin Falls/US 93 exit and turn south toward Twin Falls. Continue ahead six miles to US 30. Turn right (west) toward Bliss.

Highlights: *Beyond Bliss there is water: cold water gushing magically from walls of black-rock canyons; hot water bubbling into soaking pools; water gliding along the beautiful Snake River canyon; water irrigating miles of desert cropland. Beyond Bliss is a forty-seven-mile route through many of south-central Idaho's most beautiful places.*

On I-84, you can drive the thirty-five miles between Bliss and Twin Falls in half an hour. Please don't.

Instead, take the more leisurely, more scenic, and longer (by twelve miles) US 30, which parallels the interstate. This choice may add an hour to your travels—or, if you really enjoy the sites along the way, extend your trip by several days.

On US 30, you'll follow the route of the Oregon Trail, the pathway used by approximately 300,000 emigrants heading west during the 1840s and 1850s. The trail across this part of the Snake River plain was actually a series of parallel routes through the desert on both sides of the river. Most Oregon Trail pioneers going from the Twin Falls area to what is now Bliss used this route, which evolved into US 30.

Begin at Bliss, a small town (population 500) perched between I-84 and the Snake River canyon. Bliss has one of my favorite Idaho town names—as delightful as Hope, Sweet, and even Wilder.

Follow US 30 east from Bliss toward Twin Falls. This route has been officially honored for its enchantment with the designation Thousand Springs Scenic Byway.

When the highway meets the canyon rim two miles after leaving the interstate, the irrigated fields of alfalfa give way to the desert's most common plant, sagebrush. Even the sagebrush has a hard time hanging on as the highway drops into the Snake River canyon at milepost 175. To learn about the geological history of this canyon, stop at the viewpoint pullout on the right, just below the canyon rim.

From this pullout, note both the steep black-rock walls of the canyon's north side and the softer rounded hills to the south. The black rock is basalt, a thick lava that repeatedly oozed from cracks in the earth's surface over millions of years, to harden and then build the flat Snake River plain layer by layer. This layer cake of rock is now about 5,000 feet thick. The Snake River, which carved this canyon, was pushed south and west by the flows. The river also continues to erode the rocky cliffs on the north side. The torrent of water released by the Bonneville Flood (see Chapter 6) spurred that erosion process. Right next to the road, look for crumbling ledges of basalt, as entire sections are undercut and seem ready to fall.

The rolling sandy hills across the river from this overlook site changed many times during that period of basalt flow. New flows would push the river farther south or block its passage, creating lakes and swamps that disappeared as the river cut a channel through each temporary obstacle. Those lakes and swamps were filled with sand and silt that was either eroded from the hills above or deposited by river floods. Sometimes that filling process preserved the remains of the animals and plants that thrived there, creating a layer of fossil-bearing rock or soil. That's exactly what happened across the river from this viewpoint.

Hagerman Fossil Beds National Monument is on the far bank of the Snake River, approximately four miles upstream from this overlook and just across the river from the town of Hagerman. The 5,000-acre site, administered by the National Park Service, is now under development. Be sure to contact the Park Service before entering the site. Public access across private land is under negotiation, and in some areas unstable sand makes travel dangerous.

At the national monument, what was a lake and marshy area 2.5 to 3.5 million years ago is now the finest source of freshwater fish and small mammal fossils in North America. In addition, preliminary digs have unearthed the fossilized bones of early horses, camels, beavers, turtles, otters, and a variety of birds.

The Hagerman Fossil Beds are changing rapidly, and plans are being finalized to establish a visitors center and other amenities here. Because of the beauty of the site and the quality of the historical record, the number of visitors is projected to increase to 250,000 yearly when the national monument is fully developed.

Continuing ahead on US 30, watch for the bridge over the Malad River one mile past the viewpoint. In this steep-sided canyon, the local electrical utility, Idaho Power, has built two generation plants at the confluence of the Malad and Snake Rivers. The site, located along a remote section of the Snake River, is worthy of a picnic.

As you cross the bridge, watch for the waterfall hiding downstream in the canyon. Turn right at the Idaho Power sign, turn right and follow the gravel road if you want a quick side trip to the Snake River. The waterfall from the company's overflow channel appears immediately ahead, and during the spring the natural flow over the adjacent rock ledge increases the dramatic effect. The gravel road leads to the river and a picnic site.

Upstream on the Malad is a more breathtaking viewpoint. This site is part of Malad Gorge State Park, which is accessible only from I-84 and is the one good reason to drive the interstate in this region. At the state park, which is open only during the warm months, visitors at the vista point immediately west of the Tuttle exit on the interstate can stand at the edge of Devil's Washbowl. Here a sixty-foot waterfall cascades into a boiling pool right below the overlook site. This park also provides visitors with a picnic area, a footbridge across the ravine, and a great cliffside trail.

Back on our country road, a second Idaho Power facility, called the Lower Salmon Project, is three miles ahead on US 30. At milepost 179, just before Billingsley Creek, turn right at the sign. More potential picnicking awaits you here.

Two miles down the highway is the town of Hagerman, one of my favorite Idaho communities. Hagerman has it all. The setting is idyllic, with easy access to two rivers, four reservoirs, and even a fly-fishing stream. Many of the town's commercial structures have a wonderful Old West look—even the bank, which is housed in a beautiful rock-walled building constructed for the Stock Growers and Traders Bank in 1887. In addition to the usual small-town fare, a winery, artisans' shops, several outfitters' and guides' headquarters, and some great restaurants line the streets. The Riverbank Restaurant sells Hagerman catfish.

Before leaving the Hagerman area, make sure to visit the Thousand Springs. This is where the Big Lost River is found again. The Big Lost goes underground near Arco (see Chapter 7 for details), more than 100 miles northeast of Hagerman, and flows below the earth's surface in cracks and channels through the basalt to erupt out of the Snake River canyon walls.

The Thousand Springs were an object of wonderment to Oregon Trail travelers. Imagine their amazement, after they had walked or ridden across miles of desert, at finding fresh cold water spraying from the rocks partway down the cliffs above the Snake River. Later settlers viewed the springs in a more utilitarian manner. They harnessed most of them, using the water for irrigation, electrical power, or, more recently, raising trout in huge fish farms.

Now, because of that water use, only a few of the springs run free. Along the twenty miles of riverside cliffs where the water originally flowed, only isolated springs remain visible. The good news is that the best remaining area has been preserved by the Nature Conservancy and is open for public inspection at no charge. The bad news is that the route to this site, Ritter Island, is neither direct nor simple.

To take the side trip to Ritter Island, at milepost 183 on the far (south) side of Hagerman, turn left onto a paved road marked with a sign for the Hagerman National Fish Hatchery. Follow the hatchery signs to the second fork in this road. Here a right turn will lead to two fish hatcheries, one run by the federal government and one run by the state government. These hatcheries are open for tours, and a delightful grassy creekside picnic area has been provided for visitors' use. The adjacent Hagerman Wildlife Management Area, between the hatcheries and the Snake River, is open for hiking and limited fishing.

A left turn at that second fork leads to Ritter Island, although no sign indicates that. Continue past the fork for 3.5 miles on the main paved road. There a sign reading "Thousand Springs Hydro Project" points to the right, down a gravel road. On the left, opposite the sign, is a nice stone house and barn.

Backpackers talk with a wilderness ranger

At that sign, turn right and continue ahead one mile to Ritter Island. The gravel road winds to the edge of the canyon and then drops down toward a trout farm. In the large tanks, trout thrive in the cold water piped in from the nearby springs. Aquaculture sites around Hagerman make Idaho the nation's number one producer of commercially grown trout.

At the fish farm, turn right and then immediately look to the right, toward the canyon wall. Here one of the Thousand Springs gushes from a small cave in the basalt wall, forming a beautiful grotto of ferns and mosses and creating a stream aimed for the fish farm.

At the bottom of the canyon wall, Idaho Power, in a moment of corporate whimsy, built a generating plant that looks like a stone castle. The company also maintains a very pleasant day-use picnic area along the Snake River here.

Across the wooden bridge by the picnic area is Ritter Island. The bridge is gated, and calling the Nature Conservancy ahead to arrange for a tour, or at least an unlocked gate, is a sensible idea.

The Nature Conservancy owns all of Ritter Island, including the mansion and farm buildings around it. Tours of the mansion are available on request. Several ongoing projects are aimed at restoring the grounds to native vegetation. The springs are visible halfway up the 400-foot-tall cliff to the north of the mansion grounds.

Hiking across a riverside pasture to the northeastern shore of the island puts visitors directly opposite the springs. Here a series of springs fills a section of canyon wall about 100 feet in length. The springs spout from the wall in white-water streams that cascade down into the channel between the island and the river.

In this desert country, to see and hear fresh water bursting from black rock is a remarkable experience. Almost equal to that vista point is the island's heron rookery, where the great birds return annually to raise their young, and the 400-foot Sand Springs Falls near the southern end of the island.

After feasting on this vision of water and rock, retrace the route to US 30 at Hagerman. Turn left (south) toward Buhl.

After the highway crosses the Snake River on the Gridley Bridge, at milepost 186 look to the left, across the river, for great views of the springs by Ritter Island. A mile later, on the left, is the first of three roadside hot springs resorts. For relaxing road-weary children (and adults) these hot pools are hard to beat. The resorts offer both a large swimming pool filled with hot water and a series of individual soaking rooms for maximum comfort and privacy. Camping and RV sites also are available. Sligar's 1000 Springs Resort is the first, at milepost 187, followed by Banbury Hot Springs Resort and Miracle Hot Springs Resort, at milepost 191.

The highway soon leaves the rugged black rock of the canyon and enters an area of fertile irrigated farmland known locally as the Magic Valley. Four miles past the last two hot springs resorts, the tidy homes of the town of Buhl (population 3,500) appear. Besides agricultural productivity, Buhl's main claim to fame is Balanced Rock.

A forty-foot-tall rock does balance at Balanced Rock Park, a very nice county-maintained picnic site about fifteen miles southwest of Buhl. This large rock looks poised to fall from its narrow base. Perhaps the addition of a cement collar around the pedestal has ensured its survival. Local children and families visit the park more to enjoy the tubing and water fun on Salmon Falls Creek than to view the unusual rock formation.

Back on our country road tour, US 30 continues through fields of potatoes, onions, grain, hay, and virtually anything else that thrives in irrigated desert agricultural areas. Fifteen miles from Buhl, the highway enters the largest community in south-central Idaho, Twin Falls (population 28,000).

You'll be coming into Twin (the town's local nickname) through its present back door. Before I-84 was built a half dozen miles away across the river, US 30 was the front door. Now the main gateway to Twin Falls is the one nearest the interstate, on US 93 by the Perrine Bridge at the northern edge of town. To get to the city's front door, continue ahead on US 30 into the center Twin Falls. Turn left (north) at the intersection with US 93 (Blue Lakes Boulevard). The final stop on this country road tour is three miles ahead, at one of the finest and most attractive information centers in Idaho, the Buzz Langdon Visitor Center.

Pull into the parking lot at the visitors center for all the information on the region that you could want and for the spectacular view. At the edge of the parking lot, past the low stone wall, you can look out over a canyon 1,500 feet wide and more than 400 feet deep that has resulted from the erosive churning action of the Snake River, with two golf courses sharing the valley floor with the river. Adjacent to the same parking lot, US 93 leaps across this chasm in one graceful bound on the Perrine Bridge.

This beautiful span is a great walkway for those who want to savor this great river valley. A fenced sidewalk lines both sides of the bridge—for which I was certainly grateful on my walk across the bridge, as gusts of wind up the canyon tried their best to push me into the traffic or over the side. On the far (north) side of the quarter-mile bridge, the plain looks much as it did at the time of the Oregon Trail—just sagebrush desert and rocks.

The open land to the right (east) of US 93 is the Snake River Rim Recreation Area. A dirt road, the first right turn after the bridge, provides access to the recreation area. This huge parcel of desert land is administered by the Bureau of Land Management for free public use as a hiking and motorcycling area. Trails crisscrossing the area provide spectacular views of the canyon. Just remember to use caution, as there are no walls, fences, or warnings as you approach the abrupt edge.

From the Buzz Langdon Visitors Center, armed with answers to all your questions, you can go north on US 93 toward Sun Valley or south into Twin Falls and the many other fascinating sites in the Magic Valley.

One place that deserves a visit is Shoshone Falls, on the Snake River about four miles upstream from the Perrine Bridge. At 212 feet high, this waterfall is 50 feet taller than Niagara Falls, and during the height of the spring runoff, it carries about as much water as its more famous cousin.

Perhaps one reason Shoshone Falls is not more widely known is its temporary nature. Virtually every year, the demand for water from cropland irrigators upstream exceeds the supply, and the falls are sucked dry. Try to plan a visit to Shoshone Falls during the spring—from March to early June—for maximum dramatic effect.

Besides the obvious thrill of seeing such a large waterfall, Shoshone Falls is interesting for other reasons. The wide basin surrounding the falls was created by the erosive force of the Bonneville Flood. When Lake Bonneville (which covered much of Utah and southern Idaho) broke through the earthen dam near the present-day city of Pocatello about 15,000 years ago, the floodwaters overflowed the existing Snake River canyon and created a separate, parallel channel from Rupert to the Twin Falls area. At Shoshone Falls, the two channels rejoined, and their combined force helped create the magnificent canyon downstream past the site of the Perrine Bridge. The width of the canyon, the piles of shattered rock, and the sculpted smoothness of the canyon walls are evidence of those floodwaters.

Even the hearty salmon could not swim past this 200-foot tall barrier. Shoshone Falls marks the upstream end of fish migration in the region. Native trout species were the aquatic inhabitants of the upper section of the river beyond this waterfall.

Even summer visits to Shoshone Falls are worth the drive. Without water pouring over the falls, it is easier to see the smooth curves of the canyon and the other evidence of the flood. The City of Twin Falls maintains a riverside park below the falls.

To find Shoshone Falls, go south from the visitors center on US 93 toward Twin Falls for one mile. At Falls Avenue, turn left (east) and continue ahead for four miles. At 3300 East Avenue (watch for the small sign at this intersection), turn left (north). A nice overlook is a mile ahead, and the park is one mile farther on.

To locate Twin Falls, the double waterfall that gave its name to both the town and the county, do not turn off Falls Avenue at 3300 East Avenue. Instead continue east on Falls Avenue for another two miles, then turn left (north) at 3500 East Avenue. Twin Falls is a mile ahead. Idaho Power maintains a picnic area here, given to the public in exchange for taking Twin Falls away. One of the twins is entirely dammed, and the other is more like a series of rapids than a waterfall. If you are expecting something spectacular after visiting Shoshone Falls, you'll be disappointed.

In the Area

Bliss
Chamber of Commerce: 208-352-4293

Hagerman
Hagerman Fossil Beds National Monument: 208-733-8398 or 208-837-4793

Malad Gorge State Park: 208-837-4505

Idaho Power, Lower Salmon and Malad Projects:
208-837-6431

Idaho State Bank: 208-837-6464

Chamber of Commerce: 208-837-9131

Hagerman Valley Historical Society Museum: 208-837-6288

Rose Creek Winery: 208-837-4413

Riverbank Restaurant: 208-837-6462

Hagerman National Fish Hatchery: 208-837-4896

Idaho Department of Fish and Game State Fish Hatchery:
208-837-4892

Nature Conservancy, Ritter Island Preserve: 208-536-6797

Buhl

Sligar's 1000 Springs Resort: 208-837-4987

Miracle Hot Springs Resort: 208-543-6002

Banbury Hot Springs Resort: 208-543-4098

Chamber of Commerce: 208-543-6682

Twin Falls County Museum: 208-734-5547 or 208-733-7870

Balanced Rock Park, Twin Falls County Parks Department:
208-734-9491

Twin Falls

Buzz Langdon Visitor Center: 208-733-9458

Chamber of Commerce: 208-733-3974 or 800 255-8946

Idaho Power, Power Plant Tours: 208-423-5698

Shoshone Falls Park, Twin Falls City Parks Department:
208-736-2265

U.S. Forest Service, Sawtooth National Forest: 208-737-3200

Bureau of Land Management: 208-736-2350

10 ~

This Snake
Has Two
Forks

From Idaho Falls (south to north): Begin on I-15 at the city of Idaho Falls, which is 50 miles north of Pocatello or 200 miles south of Butte, Montana.

From Montana (north to south): Begin at the Montana border near Henry's Lake, either coming from Yellowstone National Park through the town of West Yellowstone on US 20 or headed south from I-90 on US 287 at Three Forks, Montana, then State 87. US 20 and State 87 meet at Henry's Lake at the northern end of this country road.

Highlights: *From the home of the famous Idaho potato, this 160-mile route follows both of the Snake River's main tributaries, the South Fork and Henry's Fork, to equally famous fishing, hiking, hunting, boating, and wildlife viewing. Along the way, through the majestic high country Idaho shares with Wyoming and Montana, is the valley on the back side of the Teton Range and an easy route over the Continental Divide. From moose to white pelicans, elk to eagles, this is where the wildlife lives on.*

The potatoes that fill the fertile fields from Twin Falls to Rexburg are this state's best-known product. Even the Idaho auto license plate boasts that this is the home of the "Famous Potatoes." Idaho grows more potatoes than any other state— about 100,000,000 pounds annually, one-third of the national total.

Here in eastern Idaho, along I-15, watch for row after row of spuds growing in long, tidy mounds. Water pumped from the Snake River keeps them green through the hot summer. In the early spring, the fields look like rows of small tomato plants. By midsummer, the potato vines sport small white blossoms. In the fall, the plants wilt with the first frosts, to resemble lines of blackened plant skeletons. After the cold weather has hardened the skins of this delicious tuber, the potatoes are harvested and stored in the huge half-buried sheds that dot the landscape.

Potatoes are grown all around the city of Idaho Falls (population 50,000) where this country road tour begins. But for those potato lovers who want more than a drive-by view of Idaho's best, I suggest a side trip to the town of Blackfoot, twenty-six miles south of Idaho Falls on I-15.

Blackfoot is the home of Idaho's World Potato Exposition, located at the old train station downtown. At this quaint museum, you'll have a chance to see old spud-harvesting equipment, admire the world's largest potato chip, purchase the official Idaho Potato Commission history (titled "Aristocrat in Burlap"), and, best of all, sample a hot baked potato. The museum's motto, "Free Taters for Out-of-Staters," is no empty come-on. Visitors from other states (luckily, they include travelers from North Idaho in that category) are ushered into a separate kitchen and served a piping-hot baked potato, complete with butter or sour cream. At the big tables, I met visitors from across the nation, all enjoying their snack.

Energized with spud power, turn north on I-15 toward Idaho Falls to begin this country road. Outside the freeway corridor, travel in this mountain area is difficult and dangerous in winter. The highways are maintained and passable year-round, but the heavy snows in this high-elevation country should discourage all but the most dedicated winter sports enthusiasts. For those who dare to take on the icy road conditions, wildlife viewing is often enhanced during the cold months, as moose, deer, and other large mammals seek the relative warmth of the river canyons.

The best place to begin an inspection of Idaho Falls, and the finest source of information about the region, is the Eastern Idaho Visitor Information Center. The Bureau of Land

Management, the Idaho Falls Chamber of Commerce, and the U.S. Forest Service cooperatively administer this attractive center in downtown Idaho Falls. Maps of all the nearby forests and highways, a pile of brochures and interpretive books, answers to your where-to and how-to questions, lists of guides and outfitters for land and water trips, and even U.S. Geological Survey topographic maps are available here.

This visitors center also is a good place to begin a walking tour of the city. The Snake River, which bisects Idaho Falls, is a block away. A riverside greenbelt, with a paved three-mile loop trail, encircles the town's waterfall and provides a haven for flocks of waterfowl. When flowing, the falls of Idaho Falls is a lovely sight. During the midsummer months, all the river's flow is diverted to generation of electricty or irrigation, eliminating this beautiful cascade.

A huge white building with a gold statue on top, located adjacent to the greenbelt, dominates the city skyline. This is the Idaho Falls Temple of the Church of Jesus Christ of Latter-Day Saints (a religious order commonly referred to as the Mormons). This temple is the oldest and largest in Idaho and one of only forty Mormon temples worldwide. The temple building itself is open only to LDS members, but an attached visitors center offers information about the church and access to its vast collection of genealogical records. The size of the temple complex provides an index of the political and economic power this church holds in the eastern part of Idaho. Much of this region was settled by Mormon farmers migrating north from Utah (see Chapter 11), and church affiliation continues to be very important to the area's residents.

When you're finished with Idaho Falls and ready for the open road, follow US 26 northeast. This route follows the South Fork of the Snake River toward its headwaters in Wyoming.

The first recreational option appears at milepost 352, fifteen miles from Idaho Falls. A left turn at the well-marked intersection here leads to the Heise Hot Springs Resort and the Kelly Canyon Ski Resort.

Five miles beyond that intersection, take a break at the rest area on the left for an incredible view of the South Fork. The river has carved a wide, steep-walled canyon here. This isolated valley is filled with aspen and cottonwood trees and an amazing variety of waterfowl. Canada geese, swans, herons, ducks, and even the beautiful white pelicans live here. For sixty miles, from Palisades Reservoir at the Wyoming border to the confluence with the Henry's Fork near Idaho Falls, the South Fork flows freely and majestically through this canyon.

The river valley is home to so many species of birds, mammals, and fish and it is such a pristine ecological area that the U.S. Fish and Wildlife Service has declared it the most important remaining wildlife habitat in Idaho. Float trips through this valley are wonderland journeys and can be arranged by contacting guides through any local chamber of commerce. This section of river is also a world-class fly-fishing area, with an abundance of cutthroat and brown trout. Moose, black bears, deer, and mountain goats roam the valley.

As our country road tour continues past the rest area, the river and highway soon separate. The river bulges north, and the highway leaves the agricultural area to wind along hillsides that gradually fill with trees as you climb slowly toward the Teton Range. A dozen miles past the rest area, the road drops into the valley of the South Fork and then crosses the river to enter the small town of Swan Valley (population 140).

Just before the bridge, at milepost 373, turn right for a side trip down a gravel road to one of the most enchanting places in Idaho. Snake River Road follows the south bank of the river from the junction of US 26. A U.S. Forest Service sign points to several campgrounds down this road.

From US 26, count 1.4 miles down Snake River Road to the small pullout on the left and the small sign for Falls Creek. A walk of fifty feet from the parking area down a narrow trail leads to the edge of the canyon and one of the most magnificent vistas in Idaho. Ahead is the South Fork of the Snake in all its splendor, with the riverside forests vibrant green in the summer and golden in the fall.

At your feet is a waterfall, a series of braided cataracts plunging more than 100 feet to the river. This is the Falls Creek Waterfall, one of the most beautiful and easily accessible falls in the state.

The basalt wall on the far side of the canyon provides a lustrous black backdrop to the majestic river weaving between islands. Large numbers of waterfowl, both flying and floating, emphasize the beauty of the scene. On my visit here, I was thrilled by the graceful flight of five white pelicans, twirling and circling, landing in formation, and then soaring away downstream.

To continue our country road tour, return to US 26 and cross the bridge into Swan Valley. Since this village is the only settlement for miles, all the necessary visitor services, including guiding and outfitting, are available here.

At Swan Valley, turn left on State 31. This road, officially designated the Teton Scenic Byway, climbs quickly out of the valley of the South Fork, passes scattered hay and cattle operations, and crosses Pine Creek Pass, elevation 6,720. This is a great road, with expansive vistas lurking around almost every curve.

The wide, flat valley on the north side of Pine Creek Pass is the Teton Valley. Fur trappers, the first white visitors to the area in the early 1800s, called it Pierre's Hole in honor of Old Pierre Tevanitagan, an Iroquois trapper and guide. Like Jackson Hole, Wyoming, on the other side of the mountains, the valley is a "hole," or flat plain surrounded by mountains.

White pelicans form springtime nesting colonies in Idaho

The Teton Range and Grand Teton National Park provide a magnificent backdrop to the east. It is true that the Tetons are not as spectacular from the Idaho side as from the Wyoming side, and the famous jagged peaks of the Tetons are not even visible from this route until you pass Driggs and head north toward Tetonia. Nevertheless, the mountains surrounding this round valley are wonderful. This area has not been designated a national park and thus is not as well-known or as heavily traveled as the Jackson Hole area. For this reason, the Teton Valley is known locally as the "quiet side of the Tetons."

On this high-elevation plain (6,100 feet), the primary agricultural products are hay and cattle. However, the main industry is recreation, with great hiking, camping, hunting, and fishing in the surrounding mountains, as well as resorts and RV campsites throughout the area.

At the first community in the valley, Victor (population 300), that focus on travelers' dollars is apparent on the town's main street, which is a series of galleries, artisans shops, and restaurants. When State 31 dead-ends at State 33, turn left toward Driggs, nine miles away.

Driggs, with a population of 1,000, is the big city in the Teton Valley. The town has an Old West feel, with old wooden storefronts downtown and views of the forested mountains at every turn. All traveler services are offered at Driggs, which is important since no services are available ahead for seventy miles.

Despite its remoteness, T-shirts proclaim that Driggs is "The Cultural Hub of the Universe." And given the interesting mix of artisans and adventurers here, that description is more appropriate than it may seem at first. Driggs is a fun town, and if it is anything remotely resembling a cultural hub, the center of that hub must be the Mountaineering Outfitters, Inc.

This store is possibly the most crowded and disorganized retail outlet in the state—but it is also one of the best sources of reasonably priced outdoor gear. Boxes of backpacking meals are stacked to the ceiling alongside packs, clothing, and sleeping bags. The store also functions as the area's unofficial information center, dispensing news of environmental activities as well as great places to visit.

Continuing past Driggs on State 33, you'll see the back side of the Tetons come into view to the right (east). Through the tiny farming communities of Tetonia, Felt, and Drummond, life goes on as if the residents were unaware of the great jagged peaks towering to the east. The placid rural scene along the highway is a great counterpoint to the dramatic mountain backdrop.

After Tetonia, continue on the Teton Scenic Byway by turning right (north) on State 32. Another twenty-five miles and much bucolic scenery later, this highway ends at State 47.

The town of Ashton and the intersection with US 20 are two miles to the left (west). To the right (east) is a wonderful forty-mile road along the Henry's Fork of the Snake River that is poorly maintained and often impassable during the winter. The two routes—left and right, respectively—meet again at Island Park. Contact the Ashton Chamber of Commerce or the U.S. Forest Service's Island Park Ranger Station for road conditions. If the season is appropriate and the spirit is willing, turn right and take the wilder route. If the snow is deep and the sedan rides on bald tires, turn left on US 20.

Our country road tour continues to the right on State 47. This highway goes through some of the most remote and beautiful parts of Targhee National Forest. Focusing on the area's recreational potential, the U.S. Forest Service has designated this route the Mesa Falls Scenic Byway. Plenty of campgrounds are scattered through this forest of aspens and lodgepole pines.

A stunning example of the vistas along this route is the viewpoint on the right at milepost 11. From this overlook, you'll see the valley of the Warm River in the foreground and the Tetons in the distance.

At milepost 12, in the middle of nowhere, State 47 ends. The Idaho Department of Transportation stops maintaining the road at this point. The U.S. Forest Service takes over, resulting in many more potholes and less regular snow removal. The road does continue as a paved two-laner, suited for all vehicles in good weather. Continue bravely beyond the warning sign.

Your reward awaits you within a mile. Turn left at the sign for Lower Mesa Falls Campground. Unless you are ready to camp here, follow the access road to the right, toward the overlook. Park at the wall and walk fifty yards to the magnificent view of the Henry's Fork—named for the early explorer Maj. Andrew Henry.

This river is the Snake's second major tributary (the first is the South Fork along the earlier segment of this route). The Henry's Fork is world famous for the quality of its fishing.

The overlook rests upon a loose slope of basalt boulders that cascade down to the river and sixty-five-foot-tall Lower Mesa Falls. From the overlook, you can hear and see the falls about half a mile away.

For an even more spectacular view, continue one mile on and turn at the sign for the Upper Mesa Falls Overlook. This falls is 114 feet tall, almost twice the height of its downstream neighbor. Continue down the paved access road for one-half mile to the parking area. This site was acquired by the U.S. Forest Service in 1986. Thanks to a partnership between the Forest Service and the Idaho Department of Parks and Recreation, a new state park, to be called Mesa Falls Park, will be established here.

The old log lodge by the parking lot was built at the turn of the century and will be renovated as an information center. A paved trail, about 100 yards long, has already been built from the parking lot to the river, and picnic tables and rest rooms have been constructed along the path. At the cliff above the river, a new solid boardwalk leads to overlook points that put visitors safely at the edge of the falls, although they seem closer than anyone should really get to a 114-foot-tall waterfall.

At the falls, I noted that the most common response to the sight was "Wow!" With the constant spray, narrow canyon, beautiful forest, and regular pounding of the falls, that reaction seems entirely appropriate.

After soaking in enough of that sight, continue our country road tour by returning to the Mesa Falls Scenic Byway and turning left (north). After going through twelve more miles of aspen and lodgepole pine forest, this road ends at US 20. At the junction, you can turn left to visit Harriman State Park (the entrance is one mile south on US 20). That's a side trip well worth your time.

Harriman State Park was a gift from the descendants of the railroad magnates who bought this valley as a private retreat at the turn of the century. The Henry's Fork glides through the center of the park, attracting a fantastic array of wildlife. Moose, elk, otter, deer, eagles, geese, and osprey are regularly seen at the park and throughout the adjacent 16,000-acre Harriman Wildlife Refuge. Fishing here is exceptionally good.

Wintertime wildlife watching at Harriman is especially rewarding, since the area is the cold-weather home of bald eagles and trumpeter swans. An abundance of springs keeps the river ice free to attract the eagles and swans. Cross-country ski trails provide access to those wintering sites. At any time of year, this park is considered one of the best places to see a variety of animals in a setting of amazing beauty.

Hiking and picnicking are the primary activities at Harriman State Park. Camping is not allowed. Tours of the working cattle ranch that remains here are offered during the summer.

After leaving Harriman State Park, or after leaving the Mesa Falls Scenic Byway, continue this country road tour by turning north on US 20, toward Montana and Yellowstone National Park. You will enter a community that, even by Idaho's notoriously lax standards, is unusual. This is Island Park, which describes itself as a town built around one thirty-three-mile-long street.

Bull elk spar in the fall

Calling this area of scattered homes, resorts, cabins, stores, and ranches a town seems ridiculous. It is really a forest where the number of deer well exceeds the number of human residents. But the locals insist that the area from Harriman State Park north to Henry's Lake and the Montana border—the thirty-three miles of US 20 that make up the last segment of our country road tour—is the "town" of Island Park.

Actually, this area is a single geological entity. It was a huge volcano about 500,000 years ago. Then it collapsed, leaving a caldera (a ring of hills that are the remnants of the volcano's walls) eighteen miles wide and twenty-three miles long. That oval basin filled with lava, forming a flat plain at an elevation of 6,000 feet that later was covered with trees and bisected by the Henry's Fork.

In the early years of this century, Island Park became the entrance to Yellowstone National Park. Stagecoaches chose this route because it was a relatively flat and easy way to cross the Continental Divide into Montana and reach Yellowstone. Meadowlands within the thick forest became rest stops known as parks. One of those stops was known as Island Park because it was virtually surrounded by creeks and rivers. Later, Island Park became a railroad siding, the site of the regional post office, and then the community along the entire stretch of US 20 in this northeastern tip of Idaho.

Island Park is divided into a few small settlements, which are merely clusters of homes and businesses surrounded by miles of forest and outdoor opportunities. If you want to stay in this area, you'll find plenty of accommodations, from campgrounds to resorts.

A dozen miles north of Harriman State Park, at one of those settlements called Macks Inn, a five-mile side trip to Big Springs is a good choice for visitors who are looking for something fishy. Big Springs is well named. This is the primary water source for the Henry's Fork. Here spring water wells up to form a pool and then a stream that feeds into the river. That pool is filled with huge rainbow trout, enjoying the ideal conditions created by the constant temperature of the spring water. Those fish make Big Springs a memorable sight. The U.S. Forest Service maintains a campground and viewing area here.

Returning to our country road tour, turn right onto US 20. The next major intersection is at Henry's Lake. This 6,200-acre lake is the centerpiece of the glacier-carved basin at the northern end of Island Park. The treeless hills along the shoreline slide upward into the mountains that form the Montana border. This is stark, high-elevation desert, often windy and cold, but a perfect environment for trout. At Henry's Lake, cutthroat trout weighing up to five pounds, cutthroat-rainbow hybrids up to ten pounds, and brook trout up to five pounds are regularly caught by the flocks of dedicated anglers who stay at the small resorts and cabins along the lake's north and west shores or who camp at Henry's Lake State Park.

The state park is located on the southeast corner of the lake, down a two-mile access road from US 20. The park and the fifty campsites in it are open from May to October.

Henry's Lake is at the base of the last short climb over the mountains, out of Island Park and Idaho. The ridgeline of the mountain chain a half dozen miles ahead is the border between Montana and Idaho, as well as the Continental Divide. From that crest, water flowing south into Idaho ends up in the Pacific Ocean, and water flowing north into Montana ends up in the Atlantic Ocean.

It is remarkably easy to find passage across the Continental Divide in this area. A cluster of passes are only 500 or 600 feet above Henry's Lake. When people crossed the divide on foot or horseback, such passes were prized, and the route through Island Park was heavily traveled by American Indians, trappers, and early explorers, as well as the first tourists headed to Yellowstone.

Our country road ends here at Henry's Lake. If you're continuing on into Montana, you have a choice of routes. At the fork near Henry's Lake, you can turn left on State 87 north and then take US 287 north to I-90. Or you can turn right, following US 20 for fifteen miles to the western entrance to Yellowstone National Park. State 87 crosses the Continental Divide at Raynolds Pass (6,836 feet in elevation); US 20 crosses the divide at Targhee Pass (7,072 feet in elevation).

In the Area

Blackfoot

Idaho's World Potato Exposition: 208-785-2517

Idaho Falls

Eastern Idaho Visitor Information Center: 800-634-3246

Bureau of Land Management: 208-523-1012

Idaho Falls Chamber of Commerce: 208-523-1010

U.S. Forest Service: 208-523-3278

Idaho Falls Temple of the Church of Jesus Christ of the Latter-Day Saints, Visitors Center: 208-523-4504

Heise Hot Springs Resort: 208-538-7312

Kelly Canyon Ski Resort: 208-538-6261

Swan Valley

Visitor Information: 208-483-3972

Driggs

Teton Valley Information Center: 208-354-2500

U.S. Forest Service Information Center: 208-354-2312

Mountaineering Outfitters, Inc.: 208-354-2222 or 800-359-2410

Ashton

Chamber of Commerce: 208-652-3987

Island Park

Chamber of Commerce: 208-558-7448

U.S. Forest Service, Island Park Ranger Station: 208-558-7301

Harriman State Park: 208-558-7368

Henry's Lake State Park: 208-558-7532

11 ~

The Home of Idaho's Firsts

From Salt Lake City (south to north): At Salt Lake City, Utah, follow I-15 north to Brigham City, Utah. Turn east on US 91 to Logan, Utah. Follow US 91 north from Logan for twenty miles to the town of Franklin, Idaho.

From Pocatello (north to south): At Pocatello, at the intersection of I-15 and I-86, follow I-15 south for twenty-five miles to McCammon. Turn east on US 30 at McCammon and continue on for twenty-seven miles to the junction of State 34. That is the midpoint of this country road tour.

Highlights: *The state's first town and only geyser. This 120-mile route follows the Bear River upstream from the Utah border north to Soda Springs and then south again to the Utah border and one of the river's sources, Bear Lake. Along the way, expect to be astounded by a host of natural wonders, including carbonated springs, caves, and a brilliant turquoise lake.*

Southeastern Idaho is Mormon country. The first white settlers in this region were groups of farmers on missions to colonize new areas, sent by the Church of Jesus Christ of the Latter-Day Saints (members of this religious order are commonly known as Mormons). Idaho's first town, Franklin, was established by members of this church in April of 1860.

All of the Bear River valley in Idaho, which is this country road tour, was originally settled by Mormons sent north on church-sponsored expeditions. Typically, throughout the second half of the nineteenth century, groups of Mormon families would head north from their homes in Utah in wagon

119

trains. When they arrived at the predetermined destination, they would move their wagons into a circle for protection and remove the axles. With those detached wheels, they would move the logs they needed for building and firewood.

The Mormon settlers established communities centered on family and religion. The church provided the political structure for these highly organized towns, directing the establishment of cooperatively run creameries, stores, and manufacturing enterprises. The settlers built prosperous towns with wide streets that focused on central churches.

Other Mormon settlers independently ventured north to settle throughout the Snake River plain, but the migrations into southeastern Idaho were the first, and they were the only colonizing expeditions into Idaho sponsored by the church.

By 1890, Mormons made up one-quarter of Idaho's population. Their "differentness," and the fact that a small percentage practiced polygamy, was enough to trigger anti-Mormon legislation by both the U.S. Congress and the Idaho legislature. Mormons were forbidden to vote or hold political office. It was not until 1982 that the last anti-Mormon provision was removed from the Idaho Constitution.

Now, Idaho has the second highest percentage of Mormons in the United States. The political and economic power of the LDS church and its membership throughout Idaho is well-known statewide. The southeastern corner of the state, however, remains the church's bastion. The Mormons were here first, built the first farms and towns, and are still the region's most powerful organization.

The colonizers who founded Franklin in 1860 followed the Bear River valley into what they assumed was northern Utah. Later surveys of the Idaho-Utah border placed Franklin just north of the line and gave it the distinction of being Idaho's first town.

Those settlers came here for the farmland, the timber in the mountains, and the water to irrigate their crops. They

*Designed by one of Brigham Young's sons, the Stake Tabernacle
was completed in 1889*

121

didn't come for the array of natural wonders that you will find on this country road tour, which begins at the Idaho-Utah border on US 91.

Just 100 yards into Idaho, monuments to the first residents of the town fill the Franklin Cemetery on the left. On the right is a sign officially designating US 91 as the Pioneer Historic Byway.

The first stop for history buffs is downtown Franklin. Turn right on Main Street and continue two blocks to the historic district. In addition to a park, the LDS church, and a modern community hall, the historic district includes the Relic Hall (a museum of the early settlement), the Hatch House Mansion, the Village Hall (built in 1904), and the Franklin Cooperative Mercantile building. The beehive insignia on the cooperative store symbolizes both the industriousness and the organizational stability of the settlers and their church.

The diligence of the descendants of those colonizers is apparent today in the clean and prosperous towns and in the agricultural expansion of the countryside between those communities. The wide valley floor is so filled with fields of hay and grain that farmers have started climbing up the hillsides, tilling sloping ground.

The next town past Franklin is Preston. At the junction of State 34 on the far side of town, turn right onto State 34, bound for Soda Springs.

The first of the natural wonders along this route appears at milepost 42. At Ice Cave Road, watch for the sign on the right. At the Niter Ice Cave, which is 100 yards down that gravel road on the left, you'll get a chance to walk below ground.

The Niter Ice Cave is a lava tube, an air passage within the black basalt rock that flowed up from fissures in the earth to cover this valley approximately 15 million years ago. A smooth tunnel, almost one-half mile in length, was created when the basalt cooled. The floor of the cave is firm mud, located about twenty feet below the earth's surface. The ceiling is about ten feet tall. The entrance is steep and rocky, but inside a short boardwalk has been built to keep shoes dry. The cave is wet year-round, constantly moistened by dripping water, and chilly even in summer. Bring a coat and flashlight—but no money. There are no fences, gates, or toll collectors at this cave. Almost as remarkable as the tunnel itself is the lack of control over its use.

The Niter Ice Cave was discovered by the family of John Dalton in 1898 after they filed for the 160-acre homestead that included this site. They recognized the value of a cold space in this desert environment and used the cave as a refrigerator.

The side trip to the ice cave is well worth your time. It's free, after all, and very close. But most important, the cave, with its lustrous black walls, is beautiful. And walking so freely under the earth, without fear of tiny passages or unknown holes and in such a large space, encourages even those with claustrophobia to try some exploring.

To return to our country road tour, retrace your path to State 34. Turn right (north) toward the town of Grace.

In honor of the local industriousness, you can visit another kind of tunnel—not a naturally occurring one, but one created by human hands. To take this short side trip, turn right onto Last Chance Road, past Grace at milepost 46. The paved road turns to gravel when you reach the beautiful rock-walled canyon of the Bear River. Stop at the overlook one mile from the highway, at the second canal crossing the river.

The canal system moves irrigation water from the Bear River out of the canyon and onto the farm fields. In 1916, because of years of problems with the wooden channels built to carry irrigation water around the hills along the river, the local water company decided to drill through the rocky hillside to the left of this overlook. A tunnel 12 feet wide, 9 feet tall, and 1,800 feet long was drilled by hand. A metal aqueduct was built to replace the earlier cement version. The tunnel and aqueduct are still in use today, and both are visible from this site. More than just a chance to visit a beautiful river canyon, this side trip provides an opportunity to see how hard the pioneers worked to turn this desert into a garden.

To continue our country road tour, return to State 34 and turn right (north). Four miles ahead is the junction with US 30. If you are ready for a refreshing soak, consider a short side trip to Lava Hot Springs, fifteen miles to the left (west) on US 30. If not, turn right (east) on US 30 and continue six miles to Soda Springs.

Lava Hot Springs is a town of 400 surrounding a series of developed pools filled with naturally hot water. The town offers plenty of accommodations, as well as all traveler services, a museum, and a number of attractive specialty shops. The hot water that surfaces in the area is clear and odor-free, without the sulfurous smell often associated with hot mineral pools. The public pools, which are maintained by the State of Idaho and are available for a nominal fee, are clean and inviting. This is the best developed series of hot springs in the state.

The state-owned Lava Hot Springs Foundation operates an Olympic-size outdoor swimming pool that is filled with 86°F water and open from Memorial Day through Labor Day. This huge pool boasts a half dozen diving boards of various heights. The same foundation operates a cluster of small cement pools. These shallow pools also are outdoors and are kept at much higher temperatures—from 104°F to 112°F. The small pools, to which no chlorine is added, are open daily year-round. Weary children ready to splash and dive in almost-body-temperature water and adults wanting to soak away the miles will welcome a stopover at Lava Hot Springs.

To return to the country road tour, retrace your route on US 30 to the junction of State 34. Near this intersection, the

Bear River makes a sudden turn left, switching from its westward channel through Soda Springs to head south, paralleling the earlier portion of this country road. The Bear River continues into Utah to join the Great Salt Lake.

The Bear River did not always flow south from Soda Springs. Originally, it continued west in the present valley of the Portneuf River past Lava Hot Springs to the Snake River. A series of lava flows near the junction of US 30 and State 34 blocked the original channel about 28,000 years ago. The resulting rock dam forced the river to reverse the flow of a former tributary and head south.

This tour continues upstream along the valley of the Bear River, following US 30 six miles from the junction to Soda Springs (population 3,000). The first recreational site appears on the right, just as the town begins. Oregon Trail Park was built on the shores of Alexander Reservoir by the Idaho Department of Fish and Game and the local utilities that use the power generated by the dam that created this lake. This free park is a great picnic spot and a good place to try some bird watching or boating. There's a boat ramp and a swimming area.

The park is aptly named, since the area was a landmark on the Oregon Trail. Both the hot springs (now underwater at Alexander Reservoir) and the carbonated springs were well-known by pioneers crossing this desert land. Wagon ruts from the Oregon Trail are preserved today on the edge of the golf course at this park.

On the right, just past Oregon Trail Park, turn into the U.S. Forest Service office for information on the town and the surrounding mountains. That office provides a handy town map that lists all the area's geological features.

The most obvious feature is the geyser, which bursts about eighty feet skyward every thirty minutes. This is the only man-made regularly erupting geyser in the world. It was uncorked in 1937 when a drilling crew, looking for hot water for a swimming pool, tapped into an erupting blast of cool (not hot) carbonated water at 315 feet down. The pressure builds below when carbon dioxide gas mixes with water, and, just like a shaken bottle of soda pop, it then bursts upward. The water, which has a sulfury, sweet smell, has built a mound of slimy orange rock around the geyser's base.

On the half hour and the hour, this "tamed" geyser blows its top, creating a graceful plume that lasts for five to ten minutes. A small parking area is located next to the geyser. No fee is charged.

Another free site well worth visiting is Hooper Spring, located in a grassy park ideal for picnicking. At Hooper Spring, an artesian spring bubbles to the surface within a sturdy rock shelter and then flows out toward the Bear River. The water is carbonated but not mineralized and is suitable for drinking. Visitors can just dip a cup into the spring. A local favorite is Hooper Spring water mixed with a powdered juice drink. Oregon Trail pioneers regularly praised the "soda spring" water they drank from this site.

A more modern plus that accompanies a picnic at Hooper Spring is the flowing molten slag that is dumped onto the big, gray slag mountain to the east of the spring. The Monsanto Corporation mines and processes phosphates at that factory, and the waste is melted rock that flows and glows like lava. During the day, workers regularly pour huge bucket loads of this molten slag off the edge of the pile. The slag leaves the bucket a bright red liquid that soon hardens and cools to a gray powder. Watching the slag pour is a quick lesson in man-made volcanics.

Another fantastic site, Formation Springs, is located several miles northeast of town. The Nature Conservancy maintains this natural desert oasis, where clear water flows from cavelike sources across the dry plain. This spring has been fenced off, and access is by foot only.

After seeing the various springs that made Soda Springs famous (or at least moderately well-known), continue east on US 30. After Soda Springs, the valley widens, flattens, and fills with grainfields punctuated with tidy farmsteads. The native sagebrush, originally abundant in this high-desert area (6,000 feet in elevation), is relegated to the roadsides and unplowable hills. In honor of the beauty of this route, the highway is officially known as the Bear Lake–Caribou Scenic Byway.

The first major town along the route is Montpelier (population 2,600), whose chief claim to fame is that Butch Cassidy once robbed the local bank. At the intersection of US 30 and US 89, you will be confronted with the choice of traveling to Geneva or to Paris. To continue this country road tour, choose Paris and turn right (south) on US 89.

Paris was the first settlement in this part of the valley, founded by thirty Mormon families in 1863. The names of all 120 members of that wagon train are immortalized on a bronze tablet at the Paris Tabernacle.

The tabernacle is the large Romanesque cathedral built of red sandstone in the center of town. This impressive church building was completed in 1889 after five years of volunteer labor. Unlike temples (such as the Idaho Falls Temple in Chapter 10), which are closed to all but members of the LDS church, Mormon tabernacles are meeting and concert halls that are open for public inspection.

Visitors can take a free tour of the Paris Tabernacle, one of the most attractive buildings in Idaho, daily during the summer. The original wood-paneled interior, including the original long wooden benches, remains after a century of use. Several glass cases in the foyer display artifacts from the settlers' days. The tour is well worth your time, as it affords an opportunity to see some remarkable craftsmanship.

Continuing south of Paris, past more tidy farms, you'll soon spot Bear Lake to the left. This lake is so big (77,000 acres) that it straddles the Idaho-Utah border and seems to fill all the flat space at the southern end of the Bear Valley. But its size is not what visitors usually notice first. The striking thing about Bear Lake is its color—a deep turquoise or even robin's-egg blue that looks truly Caribbean or Hawaiian. The unusual color results from the white sand on the lake bottom and the dissolved carbonates in the water. This blue jewel is even more striking in contrast to the tans and browns of the surrounding hills.

Six miles south of Paris, as the few homes that qualify as the "suburbs" of St. Charles appear, a road to the right, with a sign for Minnetonka Cave, leads to a wonderful side trip into the mountains. The U.S. Forest Service's Montpelier Ranger District administers the limestone cave at the end of this ten-mile paved road. Minnetonka is open, for a nominal fee, from mid-June through Labor Day. The Forest Service has installed steps (448 of them) and an electric lighting system, so visitors need to bring only a coat (it's about 40°F in the cave year-round) and good walking shoes for the damp stairs and pathways.

Minnetonka is the only publicly accessible limestone cave in Idaho. The cave was created as water percolating downward slowly dissolved the limestone rock. The dissolved limestone creates beautiful mineralized rock formations, a process similar to the formation of the stair-step orange rock around the geyser at Soda Springs. Minnetonka Cave contains fifteen different kinds of formations, including stalactites, which grow like icicles from the ceiling; stalagmites, which grow from deposits on the cave floor; and wide draperies, where water flows in sheets down the walls.

The lacy patterns and shimmering colors of the cave formations alone are worth the hike into Minnetonka Cave. Learning about the fascinating geological processes and seeing the equally astounding results hidden within the earth are bonuses.

If you want to try some aboveground hikes or visit the nearby campgrounds, ask the Forest Service guide for local information. If you want to continue this country road tour, retrace the route to US 89, and turn right (south) toward Utah.

But before you get settled into the rhythm of the highway, take the road to Bear Lake State Park on the left. This road provides access to the northern and eastern shores of Bear Lake. To the left of this paved road is 18,000-acre Bear Lake National Wildlife Refuge. This refuge comprises primarily cattail marshes north of the lake, which are stopovers for migrating flocks of geese, ducks, and cranes. Hiking and limited boating are allowed in the refuge.

On the right, or lake, side of the access road are the two state park units. The first portion, North Beach, offers two miles of shoreline for boating and swimming. The second unit, East Beach, which is four miles past the North Beach site, has an additional four miles of shoreline. Both sites boast little development. East Beach has some primitive campsites and drinking water, while both beaches offer picnic tables.

Bear Lake is an ideal swimming lake. The water is clear, the sandy shoreline is soft, and the shore slopes gently, making the water very shallow. This lake, more than any other in the state, offers a pleasant on-the-beach feeling to the few people who know about it.

It is also a great fishing lake, with the cutthroat trout the most highly sought angling prize and the cisco the most unusual. The Bear Lake Cisco, which is unique to this lake, is a small member of the whitefish family that is harvested in great numbers during the winter months.

Returning to US 89, continue south along the lakeshore. The brilliant blue water sparkling in the sun is a dazzling sight.

This country road tour is almost done. The Utah border is quickly approaching. For those who have been captivated by the charms of the lake and want to extend their visit, the

Bear Lake Bed and Breakfast is ideal. At milepost 2, watch for the small sign pointing uphill to this bed and breakfast. A half-mile-long gravel road leads to the lovely home built by Allen and Esther Harrison in 1974. After their children moved out, they converted four bedrooms into guest rooms. From the table (or the hot tub) on the deck, virtually the entire length of Bear Lake is visible.

The Harrisons also own a section of private undeveloped beachfront directly below the bed and breakfast. Here guests can wander amid native vegetation, swim, or lounge on the sand. If you visit this beach area, be prepared for a pleasant surprise: the sand is covered with tiny shells. You'll find billions of shells, each about one-quarter inch in diameter, in piles up to six inches high or spread evenly along the beach. The shells are the only remains of several species of snails and clams that prospered on this sandy shoreline but are now extinct. The snails and clams died about 12,000 years ago, due to changes in the mineral content of the lake water. Their shells make a great memento of the unique sights and fascinating natural phenomena found on this country road tour along the Bear River.

In the Area

Franklin

Visitor Information: 208-852-2703 or 208-646-2300

Lava Hot Springs

Chamber of Commerce: 208-776-5500

South Bannock County Historical Society and Museum:
  208-776-5254

Lava Hot Springs: 208-776-5221 or 800-423-8597

Soda Springs

Chamber of Commerce: 208-547-2600

U.S. Forest Service, Soda Springs Ranger District and Visitor Information Center: 208-547-4356

Nature Conservancy: 208-726-3007

Montpelier

U.S. Forest Service, Montpelier Ranger District: 208-847-0375

Chamber of Commerce: 208-847-3717

Paris:

Bear Lake Visitor's Bureau: 208-945-2072 or 800-448-2327

Bear Lake Wildlife Refuge: 208-847-1757

Bear Lake State Park: 208-945-2790

Bear Lake Bed and Breakfast: 208-945-2688

Index

HIKING (*cont.*)
Ketchum/Sun Valley,
82–84
Morris Creek Cedar
Grove, Elk River, 23
Nez Perce National
Forest, 44–45
Owyhee Desert, 61
Pend Oreille Scenic
Byway, 1–7
Selway Bitterroot
Wilderness Area,
30
Snake River Rim
Recreation Area, Twin
Falls, 101–102
St. Maries, 17
Teton Valley, 111
HISTORIC BUILDINGS
Cedar Street Bridge
Market, Sandpoint,
6
Franklin Cooperative
Mercantile Building,
Franklin, 122
Hatch House Mansion,
Franklin, 122
Mormon Tabernacle,
Paris, 127
Temple of the Church of
Jesus Christ of
Latter-Day Saints,
Idaho Falls, 107
Village Hall, Franklin,
122
Pythian Castle, Weiser,
51

HISTORIC SITES
Big Tree, Elk River,
24–25
Birch Creek Charcoal
Kilns, Gilmore,
75–76
Chinese cemetery,
Hope, 1, 4–5
Continental Divide, 75,
117
Franklin Cemetery,
Franklin, 122
Hemingway grave site,
Ketchum/Sun Valley,
82–83
Hemingway memorial,
Ketchum, 84
Land of the Yankee Fork
Historic Area, Challis,
87
Mormon-settled area,
Bear River Valley,
119–122
Nez Perce National
Historic Trail, 26
Oregon Trail, 68, 93, 97,
101, 125
HOT SPRINGS. *See*
SPRINGS
HOTELS. *See*
RESORTS, INNS,
and LODGING
HUNTING
Boise National Forest,
Mountain Home, 68
Elk City, 47–48
Elk River, 23–25

TOWNS and CITIES (*cont.*)
  Silver City, 62
  Soda Springs, 125
  Southwick, 33
  St. Charles, 128
  St. Maries, 17–18
  Stanley, 78–80, 87
  Sunbeam, 89
  Swan Valley, 108, 109
  Tetonia, 112
  Tetonia, 111
  Troy, 34
  Twin Falls, 93, 100
  Victor, 111
  Weippe, 32
  Weiser, 50
  White Bird, 42

VISITORS CENTERS (*See*
  also FOREST SERVICE)
  Bruneau Dunes State
    Park, Bruneau, 65
  Buzz Langdon Visitor
    Center, Twin Falls,
    101
  Craters of the Moon
    National Monument,
    Arco, 72–73
  Eastern Idaho Visitor
    Information Center,
    Idaho Falls, 106–107
  45th parallel visitors
    center, 39
  Galena Overlook, 82
  Land of the Yankee
    Fork Interpretive
    Center, Challis, 87

Lost River Ranger
  Station, Mackay, 86
Sandpoint, 6
WATERFALLS
  Elk Creek Falls, Elk
    River, 23–25
  Falls, Idaho Falls, 107
  Falls Creek Waterfall, 109
  Idaho Power site, Snake
    River, 95
  Lower Mesa Falls, 113
  Sand Springs Falls,
    Ritter Island, 100
  Selway Falls, Lowell, 30
  Shoshone Falls, Snake
    River, Twin Falls,
    102–103
  Torrelle Falls, Priest
    River, 10
  Twin Falls, Twin Falls,
    103
WILDERNESS AREAS
  Frank Church River of
    No Return Wilderness
    Area, 28–29, 38, 48
  Gospel Hump
    Wilderness Area, 38,
    41
  Hells Canyon
    Wilderness Area, 38,
    41, 55–56
  Selway-Bitterroot
    Wilderness Area,
    28–30, 38, 48
WILDLIFE VIEWING
  Blackfoot to Idaho Falls,
    106

Titles in the Country Roads series:

Country Roads of Connecticut and Rhode Island
Country Roads of Florida
Country Roads of Georgia
Country Roads of Hawaii
Country Roads of Idaho
Country Roads of Illinois, third edition
Country Roads of Indiana
Country Roads of Iowa
Country Roads of Kentucky
Country Roads of Maine
Country Roads of the Maritimes
Country Roads of Maryland and Delaware
Country Roads of Massachusetts, second edition
Country Roads of Michigan, second edition
Country Roads of Minnesota
Country Roads of Missouri
Country Roads of New Jersey
Country Roads of New Hampshire, second edition
Country Roads of New York
Country Days In New York City
Country Roads of North Carolina
Country Roads of Ohio
Country Roads of Ontario
Country Roads of Oregon
Country Roads of Pennsylvania
Country Roads of Southern California
Country Roads of Tennessee
Country Roads of Texas
Country Roads of Vermont
Country Roads of Virginia
Country Roads of Washington

All books are $9.95 at bookstores.
Or order directly from the publisher (add $3.00 shipping and handling for direct orders):

Country Roads Press
P.O. Box 286
Castine, Maine 04421
Toll-free phone number: **800-729-9179**